African Tradition in Marriage

an insider's perspective

by
Patience Turtoe-Sanders

African Tradition in Marriage

an insider's perspective

By

Patience Turtoe-Sanders

Copyright ©1998 by Patience Turtoe-Sanders

ISBN 0-9-664529-0-9

Printed in the United States of America

Contact:

Turtoe-Sanders Communications Company
P.O.Box 43481
Brooklyn Park, MN 55443
Phone: (612) 561-5585
E-mail: nyphen@aol.com

Apart from the names of the author's family members,
all other names have been changed to protect the identity of those concerned.

To my mother, Mary-Titi Akarah Turtoe, for her patience, dedication, and perseverance.

To my senior sister, Mrs. Elizabeth Okundaye, for directing me to the right path. Thank you, sister.

To the memory of my brother, Major B.S. Ejoyoma-Turtoe, for giving me a "head start." Rest in peace, brother.

To my children, Nicole and Nyphen, for giving me immeasurable joy every day.

AFRICAN TRADITION IN MARRIAGE: *AN INSIDER'S PERSPECTIVE*

Contents

Preface

All too often those born in Africa are misunderstood. Simple gestures are misconstrued as crude, uncivilized, and uncultured. To some people being different is "bad." To others, this difference arouses curiosity. If people only will take the time to listen, to study other people's culture, then they may realize that the world is smaller and more similar than they think.

This book originated from my talking to troubled foreigners (those born not of Nigerian origin) who were married to Nigerians. On several occasions, while I was trying to explain the culture, these foreigners, apart from thanking me, have asked, "Pat, why don't you write a book?" The practices written here do not tell it all; there are more. Although a majority of the people interviewed were foreign women married to Nigerians, Nigerians from Delta/Edo State in particular and other parts of the country, these practices are not limited to Nigeria. A few indigenes interviewed from other parts of Africa said they can relate to some (if not all) of these practices.

This book is written not for the world to look down on the African culture, but to promote understanding. I hope that the exposure of these practices will bring about positive changes in the African community and promote a better relationship between Africans and foreigners.

Acknowledgments

I thank God for giving me the courage to write this book. To my husband, Ernest, I thank you for your honesty. To brother Ewere Okundaye, and brother Lucky Mayor and wife, Dr. Mejebi Mayor, I cannot thank you enough for being there for me twenty-four hours, seven days of the week. To my college professor and mentor, Dr. (Mrs.) Kemi Adamolekun, who is never too busy for me, I say thank you from the bottom of my heart. Your words, "Pat, I know you can do it," were very motivating and inspiring; thanks again. To Linda Amaikwu, no words can express my appreciation for your sisterly love and unrelenting encouragement. I love you. To Gloria Boyo, Clement, Francis, Chidi, Juliet, George, Chad, and many more, I thank you all for your support and confidence.

A Brief History of Nigeria

Nigeria gained independence from Britain in 1960. Nigeria is an English-speaking country in West Africa, formerly of four regions—Northern Region, Western Region, Eastern Region, and Midwestern Region. Each of these regions has been further divided into states. The country currently comprises 36 states, with one Federal Capital Territory (Abuja). More states are still being created. Each of these states has many tribes. Delta State and Edo State were formerly known as Bendel State, created out of the former Midwestern Region.

Nigeria is very rich in natural resources: iron ore, cocoa, untapped uranium, platinum, among many others. Nigeria is known internationally for the production and exportation of crude oil. Delta State has an abundance of crude oil and also exports timber and rubber.

Introduction

In the African culture, males are revered and worshipped. When a woman's firstborn is a male child, it is seen as an achievement, and a big party is thrown. Her husband's peers shake his hands and say to him, "You are a man." But if the firstborn is a female child, the husband is disappointed; he blames his wife. The wife is also disappointed in herself; she cries. In some parts of the country a husband could say to his peers, "My wife delivered a prostitute." In the Delta and Edo cultures, each time a male is born, it is said that four children are born: the son and three women, the women representing his future wives. Generally, in public schools, males are encouraged to be serious with challenging science subjects, while girls are encouraged to study subjects such as home management and the arts because they will get married and get "lost." Girls are called W.E.E.K., an acronym for and a constant reminder that *Women Education End in Kitchen*.

The picture of male superiority is drummed early into girls. A family without a male child is regarded as a family without children, because there is no one to carry on the family name. Children are wealth. Because there is no social security, no welfare, no Medicare, children are seen as insurance for the family's future existence. No man is sterile, only women. If a woman cannot bear children, she is at fault, and the community uses this against her. She is called names such as "evil" or "witch." It is assumed that because she was bad in her previous life God has not given her children and that she is therefore paying for her sins. No empathy, no sympathy, she gets what she deserves. Her husband is not supportive; he calls her "empty," meaning empty uterus (womb). Such a woman is isolated and lonesome. She is kept at arm's length. No matter how simple or humble she is, she is never trusted. She is treated with suspicion and disrespect. Children are taught from birth to beware of her. Daughters are told not to accept presents from her, lest the barrenness rub off on them. Such a woman will do anything to have a child. She may encourage her husband to marry her niece, a cousin, her best friend, or a neighbor with the hope that the new wife will bear children who will take care of her in her old age. Female genitals are mutilated for the protection of the unborn child. Polygamy is the general practice. Single parenting is highly frowned upon. It is better to have children while married, even if one is the number ten wife. Every adult is every child's keeper, a situation that keeps children in check. Any adult can beat or flog a child who needs to be disciplined, and the child's parents will be grateful.

Lovemaking is sacred, not talked about openly. Only a man makes the overture, while a wife is expected to be conservative and be ready at all times. There is no such thing as raping one's wife. The wife is the husband's property; he can have her even if she protests. What about anal or "kinky" sex? Africans do *not* participate. When a husband dies, the wife is made to suffocate a live chicken with her thighs, and she is deprived of food for up to twenty-one days to prove her innocence.

Chapter One

Marriage Ceremony and Divorce

Marriage is celebrated with pomp and pageantry, a joyous occasion, involving both the bride and the groom's family, every mother's dream for her daughter.

In some cultures, daughters are betrothed at birth. The older the husband, the better. Though this practice is very common in the northern part of Nigeria, it is not limited to that area. The girl is groomed from birth to accept the husband without question. She is referred to the would-be husband for all her needs even from her formative years. He protects her, buys her clothes, and gives her pocket money, a situation that makes her age mates envious. A man, however, will not accept a betrothed wife from a family with a bad reputation.

In other cultures, the girl is allowed to introduce her boyfriend to her parents. This is the widespread practice today. Parents prefer their daughters to marry from the same community, to avoid the stress of having to learn a new culture and for the fear of being ill-treated by the "unknown" husband's family. When a daughter introduces a boyfriend from another culture to her parents, her father finds out all he can about the boyfriend's family and the culture his daughter will be exposed to. Fathers use different methods to get such information. This is called "looking into the future." It could be through asking questions, through overt and or covert observation of the boy and his family, or through the "Spiritual," which could be through the church psychics or "Visioners," or through African traditional psychics or "Native Doctors." If the father is uncomfortable with what he finds, he advises his daughter not to marry the man. If she insists on marrying him, a father may reluctantly give his blessing, making the daughter promise that she will not hesitate to come home in the face of difficulty; another father may refuse to attend the marriage. This "looking into the future" is not only done by the girl's father, in some cases the boy's father also does it, even if the girl is from the same culture. When I was dating Wylie, a guy from the same culture as I, he told me he could not marry me because "Native Doctors" told his father that they "saw only daughters in my future."

(He was wrong.) However, sons-in-law from other communities are now gradually being accepted, with emphasis on the consequence of ill-treating their daughters made very clear during the marriage ceremony. Wealthy parents sometimes choose spouses for their children, calling it match-making, but these parents may later regret their decision since most of these marriages don't work. "Who knows tomorrow?"

The traditional African system of marriage is known as the Native Law and Customs and is centered around the bride price. In Eastern Nigeria, the more educated the girl, the higher the bride price. Generally, court and church weddings are seen as a borrowed culture. In the Native Law and Customs system, the girl introduces her boyfriend to her father. The father tells the boyfriend to come with his parents. The boyfriend comes with his parents, who formally introduce themselves to the girl's parents and tell the reason why they are there: their son is interested in marrying their daughter. This is called engagement. No ring is involved. The girl's parents now know their daughter has a future husband and will be very protective of her. She had better not be seen with any other man, otherwise she will be disowned for not being disciplined and for bringing disgrace to the whole family.

After the engagement, the girl's father sets a date for the fiancee's parents to come with members of his extended family to meet with the extended family of the girl. On the set date, the groom's parents buy the bride's parents some presents that include a set of African clothes specially tailored for this occasion—a hat for the father, an expensive headgear for the mother, a cane for the

Marriage is a family affair.

father—as well as a keg of wine and a bag of salt to be shared with everyone in attendance. Each present is symbolic: the cloth is to cover the nakedness of the newlyweds; the cane is to stabilize the marriage; and the wine is to add excitement to the marriage. The salt is of great significance. It is believed that as food without salt is tasteless, so will a marriage be without the presentation of salt. If a groom's parents do not come with all or any of these presents, it will be assumed that they do not approve of the bride; therefore, the marriage will not take place. This indeed is particularly true in the Delta area. During my traditional marriage, my future father-in-law, a chief, versed in the Delta culture, vehemently refused to present a bag of salt, a situation that angered my family so much so that they did not want to give me "away." After much persuasion from his wives, who are Christians, and my family's threat to cancel the marriage, he eventually presented the bag of salt to the relief of everyone. He later confessed to me that he did not want the marriage to take place because he thought I was too educated for his son. He was wrong. As it turned out, Papa and I became the best of friends.

In Africa, marriage can also be performed in absence, that is, without the groom being present. For instance, a man who lives in another state or who lives abroad could request his parents to perform the marriage ceremony for him. In this case, either his father or his brother will represent him. All the groom does is indicate his intention to his family and send money to his father for the ceremony. The bride could be someone the groom has known or previously dated, or she could be someone he has never met, picked by the groom's family. It depends on the groom's request.

The marriage can also be performed without the presence of either the groom or the bride. The groom tells his family that he is interested in marrying the daughter of so-and-so. The bride tells her family that the son of so-and-so has indicated his interest. The family of the groom will then go to the family of the bride, who will then set a date for the marriage. On the set date, the groom's family will bring one of their sons to represent the groom, and the bride's family will bring one of their daughters to represent the bride. All traditional rites are performed as if both the real bride and groom were present. After this ceremony, the bride and groom are officially recognized as man and wife.

This type of ceremony is done if both the bride and groom live overseas. It is also done if an African woman marries a foreigner. For instance, if the African woman is already married to an American according to the American culture, the man will say to the wife's parents in Africa, "I am interested in marrying your daughter." He cannot say, "I am married to your daughter," because he is not yet married according to the African culture. When the man has indicated his interest, the wife also tells her family that so-and-so, an American, has indicated his interest. The American man then sends money to the wife's family, who will then make this known to the community. Another family within the community will then represent the American family. All traditional rites will be performed as if both the African and the American families were present. There will be an interpreter, interpreting the native language to the "American family," explaining step by step all that is being done and what is expected of them. This ceremony need not take place if both the African woman and the foreign husband intend to go to Africa to perform the traditional marriage. Until this traditional marriage ceremony is performed, the African woman is still "single" as far as her family and the community are concerned. The husband cannot participate in traditional ceremonies as a son-in-law. However, the situation is different with an African man. He can marry any woman from any part of the world, and she will be recognized as his wife without any formal ceremony in Africa.

A foreign marriage is not recognized until the traditional African marriage is performed.

Traditionally, in the Delta area, a marriage is not consummated until after the bride's first menstruation to make sure that she is not with another man's child . . . just a precaution. This practice is strongly enforced in this area. The man may not tell the wife outright, "I will not sleep with you until you menstruate." Oh, no. He does this in style, keeping the wife feeling undesirable. Not every Delta woman is even aware of this part of the culture because the men keep it "hush-hush." (Don't ask me why.) If not for the following experience with my former husband, I probably would not have known.

Because of the distance between us, my husband and I did not see each other for a while after the traditional ceremony, and there had been no sexual intimacy before then. The expectation of seeing each other was great. It became even greater when we finally saw each other and his first words were, "Pat, take your time; I will not rush you." I felt respected. To tell you the truth, I did not know what to expect the first day. I had always known this guy, even as a kid, but it is different when you are now "man and wife." Anyway, the man kept to his "no rush" promise, or so I thought. Even though I had expected no intimacy at this time, I did expect to be touched, cuddled, you know, things like that, but no, this guy was practically running away from me! He kept saying, "Pat, I know you are shy." I am in no way a shy person and he knew it, so what was this thing about being shy? I pondered.

After some weeks, I became very concerned. I confided in an older friend, Emily. Emily and I went to the department store where she helped me pick out a very sexy nightgown and a sweet-smelling perfume. Emily instructed, "After giving him his supper, take a nice bath, spray this perfume all over you, put on this nightgown, go to him and say, 'Look at my nightgown, isn't it beautiful? I bought this for you.'" I did as Emily instructed. Did I get the expected response? When he saw me in the nightgown, without waiting for me to speak, he said, "What is this, don't you have some pride?"

My spirit was crushed. I just could not take it anymore. I informed my family, telling them that my husband does not want me to be with child. Then my family explained this part of the culture. "Then why did he not come outright to tell me? Why make me feel undesirable and unwanted?" I asked them. They responded, "You wait. After three or four months, tell us if you still feel that way."

Other women interviewed told similar stories. In this culture, if a new wife does not menstruate after one month, she is sent back to her parents because it is assumed that she is with another man's child. This is very shameful to her family. No one puts into consideration that she could be having hormonal changes.

The traditional marriage ceremony is a very long process. In some cultures it takes a whole day or two. During this ceremony, both the family of the groom and the family of the bride have a "Speaker" on each side. The Speaker from the girl's family will ask her if she really wants to marry this man, pointing to the fiancee. If she says "yes," then the Speaker from the groom's family will ask the groom if he is ready to be a "man." If the groom says "yes," then his Speaker will pause and give the groom a very long, stern look and almost immediately become melodramatic. Pointing to the groom, he will ask, "Do you know what it takes to be a man?" Without waiting for an answer, he continues, "Being a man is more than putting your 'thing' in her 'thing,'" pointing to the bride. "It means being able to say NO to your mother"—he pauses to look in the groom's mother's direction—"to defend your family, to control your wives" (with emphasis on the plural), "to provide and care for your children. My son, being a man is a whole different ball game." The Speaker continues on a tirade of the things expected of a man according to the African culture and asks the question again, "Are you ready to be a man?" If the groom says "yes," then everyone will shout for joy, and the bride will be made to sit on the thighs of the groom. The bride's father will pour libations to the ancestors asking them for guidance, direction, and blessings on behalf of the newlyweds. After this, he gives an ounce of the hard liquor (with which he had poured libation) to the groom, who will then drink one half and give the remaining half to his bride. After this drink, the bride and the groom automatically become husband and wife. Everyone cheers and the dancing begins. As the bride dances, she will be "sprayed" with money. There is a slight variation of this ceremony from culture to culture, but in all African cultures no marriage certificate is given at the end of this ceremony and no court wedding or church wedding is necessary.

Following the ceremony, the wife is then "escorted" to the husband's home. This escorting is a period of showing off all that the man has bought for the wife. Even if

Being a man is more than putting your "thing" in her "thing."

she has worked all her life to accumulate these belongings, the husband takes the credit. At this time, all her
properties are loaded in a car or two, in a van(s) or a
truck(s), including all opened and unopened marriage
presents. The bride, in her very beautiful African outfit,
is put in front, then her age mates line up directly behind
her, her club mates follow (if she belongs to any club),
then her mother's age mates and her mother's club mates
all line up, singing her praises, with the cars containing
her belongings driving very slowly behind these women.
This is a very beautiful sight to behold. Everyone will
shout, "Here she comes!" In the Delta area, there will be
a spokeswoman who will say, "Look at her, isn't she

beautiful?" All the other women will answer "eee...eee...ye." The spokeswoman, who is the mouth-

Women getting ready to "escort" a bride to her new home.

piece, will pick each part of the body, beginning from the head to the toe, and analyze it. The other women will chorus, "eee..eee..ye. Look at her head, 'good head,' round and beautiful, full of hair" (even if she doesn't have hair), "eee..eee..ye." A "good head" means a head that will bring good luck to the husband, for the people believe that some heads are jinxed. The spokeswoman goes on and on. "Look at those ears, perfectly shaped for listening to the husband." Chorus, "eee..eee..ye." "Look at those eyes, big and beautiful, mesmerizing. Can a man ask for anymore?" Chorus, "eee..eee..ye." As the bride is being praised, she is expected to respond by making *iyanga*, i.e, showing off each one, until the bride and the women in procession arrive at the home of the groom, who will be waiting with his age mates. If the groom's home is far away from the bride's, the bridal procession will take a van(s) or cars, stop a few blocks from the groom's house to form a line in the order described above, and begin making a "noise" to announce their arrival. At the groom's house, the party continues all night.

In order for the bride to change her status from single to married at her place of work, she needs something to show that she is now married. The husband accompanies her to court to swear an affidavit of marriage. This affidavit is accepted in all work places and other places in the country, except at some foreign institutions. This affidavit of marriage is, in effect, as valid as a court or church marriage certificate. A woman cannot get this certificate unless accompanied by her husband or her husband's father, with proof of marriage, such as witnesses and pictures.

Some couples, however, after performing the Native Law and Customs ceremony, also do either the church wedding or the court wedding or both, but most of these men do not honor their vows. Some men say they do the Western wedding just to make their wives happy. The vows, they say, are just words. A few men, however, take their vows seriously. The African tradition and beliefs make it very difficult for these men to honor their vows. They may start out with the right intention, but gradually become influenced by the deep cultural beliefs as they grow older. They find themselves practicing the things they had initially criticized.

It is a very common practice, for example, for a man to have many wives, with lots of concubines and twenty, thirty, or more children. In ancient times, men married many wives to have lots of children to help on the manual farm. Today, things are different. Farming is no longer the main occupation. So why do they keep marrying many wives? The number one excuse: "Since there are more women than men, someone has to marry them."

Married men are also encouraged to have extra-marital sex. Sports is not a very popular pastime, even where there are gyms they lack equipment, and entertainment centers, if any, are very few and expensive. As a result, young women, especially students, are often used to entertain senior officials of government and private firms on tours. Some workers even proposition females for their married male bosses in order to curry favor and or to get promoted. Nothing like a sex scandal involving an official in high places exists. "How else can an official show his prowess and popularity without having a 'chain' of girlfriends?" A woman who comes out to say that she was a mistress of a senior official in order to discredit him will be booed. Even her mother will *tufia* (spit) on the woman's head for bringing disgrace to the family.

With the majority of books and novels outdated, expensive, and beyond the reach of the ordinary man, social conversations generally revolve around the number of women one has slept with, who has slept with whom, and which woman is next to be "conquered." A majority of the jobs in Africa start at 8 a.m. and end at 4 p.m. The men have lots of leisure time, with little or nothing to do.

Divorce also involves the extended families of the parties concerned. There is no custody battle. The children automatically belong to the husbands. If the man lives in another culture where child custody is determined differently, he will let his wife go with the children. If the mother does not want him to lay his eyes on the children, though he hurts, he will diligently pay child support and respect the mother's wishes and wait: for the people believe that "blood is thicker than water" and that the African child is never "lost." The child will always come looking for his/her "root," no matter how much the mother maligns the father. In very few and rare cases, some men, in order to dodge responsibility, allow the women to go with the children. Traditionally, in divorce cases, the man's relatives come to the home to move the wife away, seizing all her properties. She is driven out of their "brother's" home empty-handed. They say to her, "Go the way you came, you witch." It doesn't matter if she built or contributed to building the home, if she was the breadwinner of the family, or if she helped in "making" the man. All she worked hard for is taken away from her. In some cases, the woman is beaten up and thrown out in her "birthday suit" and may be clothed by neighbors.

Traditionally, when a man does not want a woman anymore, he requests a meeting with the wife's extended family members to set a date for him to come and collect the bride price he had paid. On the set date, the husband gathers his extended family members together to meet with the wife's extended family members, and a spokesman from the husband's family will make a request for the bride price. This is done very quietly. It's a gloomy occasion, almost mournful. Until the bride price is refunded, the wife will be regarded as still married to the husband and she cannot remarry. If, however, she does remarry, she will be cursed. If, on the other hand, the man does not want a woman, and her family is willing to refund her bride price but the husband is not willing or refuses to take it, the woman can remarry and she is free of any curse. In the Delta area, if a man has collected his bride price but wants to remarry his ex-wife, the wife is made to confess all the men she slept with during the divorce. It is believed that if she does not confess and the husband eats the food she cooks or sleeps with her, the ancestors will kill him.

Chapter Two

Polygamy

Polygamy is a power issue. It is also a proof of virility. In fact, it is a woman's pride to know that her husband is virile and productive. Some wives even proposition women for their husbands. This does not in any way mean that they do not love their husbands—far from it. It only goes to show loyalty and respect for the husband. In some cultures a woman who protests or questions polygamy is branded "evil, a misfit," and all her sisters are treated as rebels and generations of women after her. Her mother is ridiculed by all, especially by the mother's female counterparts. She is blamed for not bringing up her daughter properly. When one's daughter is regarded a rebel, it is expected that the mother will gather the male members of her husband's extended family and the male members of her own extended family to protest her innocence and to disown her daughter. In the mother's words, "You all know that I did not bring up my child to be a rebel. She has become one out of her own will. I completely remove myself from what she is doing; my hands are clean. Today I have disassociated myself from her. She is on her own." Response from both families will be, "*Iyawo* (our wife) and daughter, you are exonerated this day."

To marry a second wife and subsequent wives, a man needs the permission of his first wife, not out of fear but out of respect. In most cases, however, the wife has no choice. The man sets the stage by first discussing his intention with his extended family members. The extended family members in turn become excessively nice to the wife. They visit her more frequently, shower her with lots of presents, and help her with all her household chores. The husband, in turn, "pampers" the wife, provides for all her needs and more, makes her feel special, and showers her with accolades of all sorts. He begins, "The wife of my youth—my one and only wife— my beautiful and most precious jewel." He goes on and on showering her with accolades on different occasions, whether deserved or not. Some husbands go to the length of giving their wives Chieftaincy title. Then, "My wife, you work too hard. It is time for me to bring in someone to help you with these numerous household chores, to take care of you and me and the children, to give you a break." If the wife says, "Oh, I am not complaining." He responds, "But I feel very bad seeing you work so hard." If the wife suggests getting a maid, he says, "A maid is not permanent. You need permanent help. If you are not satisfied with her, you can send her away at any time" (thus giving the wife power; so shall it be that when the wife is not satisfied with the second or subsequent wives, she has the right to send them packing). When the man finally tells his wife his intention, the wife is expected to ask if he has found a woman or if he expects her to find him one. In most cases, the man has found a woman, who he then introduces to the wife. If the wife disapproves of the "fiancee," the man will not marry her. But if she does approve, he goes ahead with the marriage ceremony with the first wife in attendance. At the ceremony, songs of praises go to the first wife, with every woman in the gathering cheering her and kowtowing to her.

The second and subsequent wives must obey the first wife. The new wife calls the first wife "Mama," "Aunt," or "Chief," but dares not call her by her first name, otherwise she will be viewed as being insubordinate, in which case she will pay a fine or be sent back to her mother to learn how to "marry." With the arrival of the second wife, the first wife no longer does any household chores. The new wife does everything, like manually washing all the clothes in the family, both the first wife's clothes, the husband's and his relatives and all the children in the family. The new wife serves food first to the first wife, who will determine if the food is good enough to serve "her" husband and the remaining members of the household. The first wife calls the husband, "my husband." The second wife calls him "our husband." It does not matter if the new wife is a career woman, young or old, rich or poor, she is subordinate to the first wife.

The first wife is expected to teach the second and subsequent wives how to marry and stay married. First wives are very powerful. They are treated as queens. If the second wife shows any sign of disrespect either verbally or by gestures, she will then be rejected and sent packing. She will be isolated even by her own family members. The first wife has the right to keep all the children in the family. In fact, she is called "Mother" by all, while her step-children call their mothers endearments such as "Sister" or "Sissy" or "Auntie."

The first wife also intervenes when there is a problem. The husband listens when she "knocks." The husband considers the first wife his confidant. He trusts her, he tells her his innermost secrets, he makes his plans with her. He lets her know that he is a human being with weaknesses. He lets her reign, he lets her control. She is the queen, held in very high esteem. She calls the shots! Disobedience to her is disobedience to the husband. She is his mouthpiece. All the other wives run to her. She is even more revered than the husband because she can send any of the other wives packing at any time and has the power to make the husband marry other women.

There is no such thing as statutory rape in the African culture. If a woman dates a younger man, she is mocked, called names, "frustrated," "old goon." All her sisters are harassed. Some people go to the extent of appealing to her mother to "beg" her daughter to stop making a fool of herself. But a fifty-year-old man can easily marry a ten-year-old girl without problems. There is no limit as to the number of these girls he can have. He can marry two women the same day; the one whose bride price was paid first becomes the senior wife.

It is further believed that if a first wife puts a curse on the husband, the curse will be effective because a first wife and the husband have the same *Ori* (head or destiny). She opened the way for the man; she is the key to his success. It does not matter if the man is rich or poor. Success, in most cases, is judged by the number of children in the family. It is also believed that a man who marries another wife at the objection of his first wife will find no peace, and that the new wife will breed "bad seed" (bad children).

Chapter Three

Children

In the Delta Urhobo area, when a child is born, the father dips his index finger into an ounce of the local liquor called *Ogogoro* and rubs it on the lower lip of the child. This is believed to make the child *Ogbeju*, that is, wiser, and to be alcohol tolerant. In Africa, children are regarded as wealth, as a future investment. The more women and children a man has, the more virile he and his community think he is. Each wife in a polygamous home competes with the others to have the most children because she wants to prove that her husband sleeps with her more than with any other. "Sleeping with" is synonymous with love. The proof is in being pregnant.

Having many children also spun out of the fear that not all children will turn out to be successful and the hope that at least one out of many will.

The average child has many names, at least three and up to six first names, with at least one very long name for "spiritual protection." For it is believed that the enemy will first of all tempt those with short names before tempting those with long names, and that before he finishes pronouncing the long name he will be worn out. Imagine trying to pronounce *Ejimetederimemikighu* (in the Delta area this means "destiny") or pronouncing *Oritsegbubemidedefenefenenalieyeweren* (this means "God has answered all my prayers"). African names, whether traditional or foreign, are usually meaningful and, in most cases, associated with the events that happened prior to conception, during conception, or at birth: *Amujirundedefenefenetoteshe* means "Let us forgive all his sins"; *Onoriode* means "Who knows tomorrow?" The name may be short and meaningful, too: *Ayo* means "joy"; *Ogaga* means "hard" (difficult); *Ola* means "wealth"; *Suru* means "Patience"; *Owumi* or *Owunmi* or *Sunki* means "love" (*Ina sunki* means "I love you"); *Akpan* means "first son"; and *Ada* means "first daughter."

It is also the belief of the people that nothing happens fortuitously, that before anything happens in the physical, it must first manifest itself in the spiritual realm. "For every happening, there is a reason," an inexplicable force always linked to the spiritual. Having many names is like having many guardian angels; therefore, if one's enemy calls one's name to do evil, one can get rid of that name and still has other names to fall back on, without losing one's guardian angel. It is easy to know if one's name has been "polluted." That name never brings good luck. Although one has many names, one must keep each name pure and out of trouble. If because one has many names one uses any or all of the names to commit a crime, then one loses one's spiritual protection. In that case, the enemy has the permission of the ancestors to do to one as the enemy pleases.

There is no such thing as an illegitimate child. "Who defines illegitimacy?" the husband will ask. "What makes the child illegitimate. Is it not as you, the wife, got pregnant that the mother got pregnant. Or is it not as you, the wife, delivered your child that the mother delivered her child? 'Illegitimate' is a borrowed word," the husband will conclude. He then goes further to give the wife a stern warning never to use that adjective on his child ever again, and so shall it be. The man has spoken. A man has the right to bring in any child to his home, and he expects his wife to keep that child without question.

The women I interviewed told several stories ranging from women dropping off newborn babies at their door steps with only one statement, "That's your husband's baby," to the husband bringing in teenagers to the home saying, "This is my son." Azogini said, "I thought it was a joke when my husband walked in with this huge six-teen-year-old and announced he was his child. He did not prepare me, nothing. I had been married to him for six years, and there had been no mention of this kid or any other kid. So when he walked in to say, 'Azee, this is my son, Philip,' I just started laughing. Believe me, I thought it was a joke, but it was no joke." Whenever a man introduces a child as his, adoption is automatic, no papers are required.

Shaking her head from side to side, another woman, Fumilayo, said, "If it hadn't happened to me, I would have thought it was a tale, or fiction from a book or something. Here I was, just returning from the hospital with my newborn baby, tired, exhausted. All I wanted to do was to sleep. Sitting by our doorstep was a woman carrying a 'bundle' on her lap. Getting closer, I realized the 'bundle' was a baby. I could not recognize the woman. I thought she lost her way or something. I asked my husband, Tade, who that could be. He exclaimed, 'Oh, Gad,' or something like that. I did not read any meaning to it. I thought she was a beggar or something, judging from the way she dressed. As soon as we alighted from the car, the woman came running towards us screaming, ignoring my presence, looking at Tade, screaming at the top of her voice, 'You think I won't find you? You impregnated me and ran away! You think I won't find you, eh, eh. Answer me, you stupid man! Well, here is your child.' The woman then handed the baby to Tade, who just stood there, frozen. I almost passed out. All the neighbors were out, looking. I didn't know what to do. When Tade wouldn't take the child, the woman started screaming all over again. 'Foolish man, won't you take your baby, or are you afraid of your wife? You were not afraid of her when you were sleeping with me with your long penis, were you?' At this point she put the child in the car and promised to come back to 'deal' with Tade. She left. I have never been so embarrassed in all my life. The child and my daughter looked so much alike, you could tell they were relatives. I could not believe it. As if nothing has happened, Tade said, 'Won't you bring the children in?' So I have children now. Incredible." She stopped, shaking her head from side to side again, and with tears in her eyes, Fumilayo said, "It's like a tale, isn't it? It happened. It happened to me, Pat, and we've only been married fifteen months."

Who defines illegitimacy? A woman is expected to treat all of her husband's children as her own.

Other women told stories of how their husbands' concubines dropped off their children with the wives, because the husband was not providing child support. In this country, there is no method of tracking child support. Taking care of your children is a matter of the man's discretion; no one will make him.

Children are taught to respect their seniors. Greeting is a big deal. When a child sees an adult, he/she is taught to greet, "Good morning sir/madam" or "Good evening, sir/madam" or as the situation demands. This custom surprised Keke's children, nine and eleven years old, respectively, visiting from America. They asked their mummy, "Why does everyone here greet everyone?" "Because it is the right thing to do" answered their mother. "What makes it right? It's nobody's business," answered the nine-year-old girl. "In Africa, it is everybody's business, now shut up!" replied the aunt who has lived in Africa all her life, posing for a showdown. If a child so much as raises his/her hand to hit the parent(s), a passer-by will beat the child so badly that the child will never hit the parent nor anyone older than him/her again.

Children are taught to worship their fathers, that fathers never go wrong. Even if a woman is the breadwinner of the family, it will be kept secret, under lock and key. The woman will never allow her child to talk back to his/her father. She worships and respects her husband; anything he says, she does. If a child therefore is stubborn to his father, he gets nothing from his mother. She will secretly (without the knowledge of the father) feed him, but deprives the child of all other essentials, according to his/her father's orders.

It is a common practice for a woman to give all her earnings to the husband; the husband in turn gives the wife pocket money or spending money and may dictate what she buys with it. It is un-African for a woman to know how much a man earns. It is believed that knowing how much he makes breeds contempt and is disrespectful to his manhood. All the money in the family is therefore controlled by him. The child is kept in the dark as to the family's finances. The impression is that the father is the sole provider. In some cultures, if a child asks for money from his mother, rather than giving the money to the child, the mother secretly gives the money to her husband and refers the child to the father, who in turn censors whatever the child needs and gives part of the money to the child. If, however, the father is not satisfied with the child's explanation, he confiscates the money and keeps it. It is very common in polygamous homes to find children from a particular woman appearing to be more favored than the others. This breeds jealousy and division among the children, who do not know that it is not actually the father who provides for these children, but their mothers through the father.

The average African man is trustworthy. He does no drugs. He has a great tolerance for alcohol. I do not know if it is the *ogogoro* or if the alcohol content here is stronger. Local alcohol, such as *Burukutu*, *Ogogoro* and *palmwine*, is the most affordable and very commonly used. There are different variety of beers, but the man prefers Heineken and Guiness Stout. The average man can drink 2880 cc of beer (a dozen 8 ounce bottles) on the spot, without any obvious sign of intoxication. He will still have his senses intact, no slurred speech, no wobbly movement, nothing. Unless he tells you how much he has drunk or you use the breathalyzer test, you will never know. He has the same level of tolerance for liquor. He can mix different liquors together without appearing to be intoxicated. It's okay for a woman to drink one or two cans of beer, but better if she doesn't drink at all. A woman who drinks like a man is labeled a drunkard even without appearing to be intoxicated. A few men surreptitiously do marijuana, because marijuana is considered a social disgrace, a stigma. It is believed that marijuana make people crazy, psychotic. So if one's child is known to do marijuana, neighbors say to one another, "Run away from that family. They are crazy. They do *igbo*." (*Igbo* is the local name for marijuana.) Here it is believed that mental illness is precipitated by *igbo*, with no cure. No one wants to be associated with such a "crazy" family. A majority of the men have never seen nor tasted "crack" or cocaine or heroin.

The African man is a good man. He does not curse; he uses words appropriately. He is very hardworking and very family oriented. The African man can work up to and beyond 100 hours a week to care for both his immediate family and his extended family members. It doesn't matter where he is, he never forgets his people. If he lives overseas, for instance, he sends money home through friends, Western Union or through Moneygram. He never forgets where he came from. He is exposed to responsibility very early in life. He believes in discipline. There are cases where male teenagers deny being the father of a pregnant female's child. Such denial is usually temporary. These male teenagers usually come back with remorse to claim their children. The denial, in most cases, is out of peer pressure and the fear of being reject-ed by their fathers.

The African father does not shy away from his responsi-bilities. He makes sure that he provides for the basic needs of his wife and children. Even if he does not have the money, he makes sure that his wife works, farms or does petty trade, just to keep the family going. He makes sure his children are never idle. He is conscious of the fact that "an idle mind is the devil's workshop." He del-egates responsibilities among his children, always keep-ing them busy. Household chores such as cleaning, cooking, fetching water from the well or spring, and babysitting are duties of the female. Security, splitting firewood, hunting, fishing, skinning animals or barbecu-ing, farming and protecting the females are the responsi-bilities of the male. The males take the responsibility of protecting their sisters very seriously. "Sister" does not necessarily mean having the same parents. It could refer to cousins, close or distant, to aunts, or an in-law. You don't "mess" with the African sister. The "brother" is like an elephant; he never forgets and he never forgives.

Age is more respected than wealth. The general practice is to call any older female "Aunt," if male, "Uncle." Teachers are called "Miss" or "Mr.," "Aunt" or "Uncle," respectively. Calling an older person or calling one's parents-in-law by the first name shows disrespect and the lack of a proper upbringing, same as using one's left hand to serve. A child is taught to stop whatever he/she is doing to give a helping hand to an older person in need, to give up his/her seat for an older person. The extended family system is very well respected and appreciated. If one person is from a village, the whole village is automatically related. Everyone is everyone's keeper. A neighbor will feed a hungry family out of the goodness of his/her heart, expecting nothing in return.

Babysitting is a pleasure for everyone. Parents babysit, neighbors babysit, cousins babysit, without asking for a dime. They may even get angry if offered money to babysit. "Why will anyone take money to babysit children?" the locals will ask. "No amount of money can replace such a pleasure." Most of the time, poor parents allow their children to babysit in exchange for the baby's family teaching the babysitter a trade or sending the babysitter to school. No direct cash is involved. Any adult can correct and discipline any child. Every neighbor watches out for the neighbor's child. This makes the child conscious of his/her actions at all times. The man may have many children, but he strives very hard to keep in touch with all of them. Even if he does not have the money, he compensates with lots of visits and asking about their welfare. However, because of the master-servant relationship between father and son, most of the sons prefer to confide in their mothers. According to one interviewee, "The average African father does not listen, he just 'barks.'"

Up to today, pregnancy and due dates are kept secret for fear of being bewitched. Some African women are so good at keeping their pregnancy secret that they will tell no one, not even their husbands, nor will they attend prenatal clinics until it's almost time for them to deliver. According to Samantha, a Liberian, "On two different occasions that I announced my pregnancy, I had miscarriages. It's like I was being bewitched or something. This time around, I told no one, and see . . ." (pointing to the baby). Some women may even deny being pregnant to very close friends and relatives but will announce the delivery, a situation that brings quarrel among friends and relatives and reaction such as "Was she pregnant?" from colleagues. Keeping the pregnancy secret or denying being pregnant is not out of distrust or suspicion of the friends and relatives but for spiritual protection from her enemies and her personal demons. When you ask an African woman her due date, it is not uncommon, therefore, for her to respond harshly, "Why do you want to know?"

Until recently, children did not know the age of their parents, neither did parents tell the age and number of children they have, because of the superstitious belief that telling the age or number of children will quicken one's death. This is still true in the rural areas today. The number of children one has are counted in terms of objects. For instance, if you ask an African person the number of children in the family, if there are ten children in the family, he/she will respond, "I have ten sticks." The sticks refer to the number of children. When the parent dies, however, his/her age will then be announced by the brother, uncle, or any older member of the parent's family. The child will first get to know the age of the parent at his/her death. In the major cities, however, things are beginning to change.

In the Western Region, though, age was not kept a secret. These people have a long history of early expo-

Children from a small African family.

sure to education. As a student at the University of Ife in the '80s, I was amazed at how parents talk very freely of the ages of their children. Even some of my classmates knew the ages of their parents. I was more than surprised. All my life I had never been so exposed. It is not as if I went to college from high school. I had previously spent three years in a post-secondary school and spent one year in the Northern Region doing a National Youth Service, a government requirement for college graduates under thirty years old. No one had blatantly talked so openly about their children's ages.

At first I was very apprehensive and scared for the children; I thought that they were going to die. But my fears soon dissipated when nothing happened to those involved. People here talked boldly about the number of children and siblings they have. My first experience was with Tunde, a classmate who asked me how old my parents were. "I beg your pardon?" I replied scornfully and with anger, too. Tunde responded, "Pat, what have I said wrong? I only asked how old your parents were." I said, "Why are you asking? Do you want to kill them, or don't you know that if I told you their age they will die?" Tunde stopped dead in his tracks, looked at me, and asked, "What?" in disbelief. "You heard me," I replied. Tunde just burst out laughing. He laughed so hard that tears started running down his cheeks. I could not understand why he was laughing, and this reaction angered me all the more. "What's so funny?" I screamed. "Don't you know that by telling their age the devil will hear and he will start counting and take them prematurely?" Tunde said, "Pat, you can't be serious." "Oh, yes, I am," I replied, stone-faced. Tunde, trying to control his laughter, said, "We've got to talk."

The next day it became a joke in the whole class. I do not know if it was the joke that did it, or if it was the experience of having almost everyone talk about it so freely. I just found myself talking about the number of children my parents had, my ordinal position in the family, and was even bold enough to ask my mother how old she was. Though Mama did not know, she gave me a rough idea of the period she was born. I asked her younger brother, who is comfortable, more educated, and exposed, but he said that he thinks I am mixing with the wrong crowd of people. He said, "Don't you students have better things to do in school than to talk about your parents' age?" He continued, "You were sent to school to learn, now go back and get busy. What your parents' age has got to do with passing your exams, I don't know." Then he gave me a long and stern look that sent cold running down my spine.

But I wasn't deterred. I went to my mother's uncle, also educated, and asked about my mother's age. He didn't know either, but he associated her birth with the death of his father (my mother's grandfather). According to my grand-uncle, my mother was six lunar months old when his father passed away. Though my grand-uncle remembered the year, he was sorry that he could not give me the real month and day. I told him he has done more than enough; at least I have a rough idea. Then I asked,

"What year was I born?" Without mincing words, he responded, "January 10, and two years after our country's independence." I said, "Yes, this coincides with what my mother and senior sister said, though differs from my teachers." As if to let me know he was abreast of things, he added, "I heard what you did with your white cloth." Seeing how surprised I was, he started laughing.

Previously, in a majority of the parts of the country, children's ages were not recorded; rather, birth was based on lunar months and associated with major events that happened that year, such as eclipse of the sun, civil war, independence of a nation, presidential inauguration, death of a prominent member of the community, to mention a few. In the Delta area, for example, dates were counted in stones and months associated with colors. January, being the first month of the year, was associated with white indicating purity; therefore, January the 10th would be 10 stones put in a white cloth and kept in a wooden box made specifically for that child.

At schools, teachers had the right to give a child any age they think the child is. Therefore, precocious children were given older years than non-precocious children of the same age group. At the time, no one took into consideration early/late bloomers or the child's mental age or IQ. All children were treated the same, undermining what the mother said was the child's age. Where the age of an individual is not recorded, an Age Declaration is given in court. This Age Declaration serves as the birth certificate and it is officially accepted. An individual cannot declare his/her age, except accompanied by the parent(s) or by an older sibling.

To age is to take pride. African women do not conceal wrinkles. Wrinkles are beautiful, synonymous with wisdom, same as gray hairs. The average African woman believes in natural beauty, no face-lifting or face-grafting or plastic surgery, no make-up. We have our own make-up, our own soap, our own creams and lotions, made from pure natural herbs, grown naturally, without preservatives. Our "Lila" lipstick is non-stick lipstick; our "Tiro" eye liner glitters and does no damage to the eyes. Some of our body oils are made purely from the coconut fruit, cocoa fruit, palm kernel and trees. All our make-up, creams and *sosorobia* perfume last all day, without adverse side effects to any parts of the body or any fear of increasing wrinkles or aging. We eat pure, natural food, grown without preservatives, no additives, cooked from "scratch," and it reflects on our skin. We are proud of our skin, proud of our heritage; we will not trade these for any amount of money in the world. As we say in my mother's tongue, *Dudu Yemi* ("I am black and proud"). And as the old people say, "If you do not know where you are coming from, how can you know where you are going?"

It would be incomplete to talk about children in Africa without talking about breast-feeding. Breast-feeding is natural; it is our pride. Everyone does it, literate and illiterate women, career women, market women and even young teenage mothers. It is done in the open without shame. Only a few women can afford a nursing brassiere. A majority of women raise their blouses and whip out the breast to breast-feed the baby with joy. No one raises an eyebrow, because the breast is doing what it is meant to do—feed the baby. The average African is breast-fed for at least one year. My mother breast-fed her last-born until the child was wise enough to say to my mother, "Mama, please keep your breast. Everyone is laughing at me that I am too old to breast-feed." She was thirty lunar months old.

When I delivered Nicole, I could not breast-feed her because she was premature, weighing fifteen ounces at birth (oh, yes, less than a pound). She could not coordinate sucking and breathing, and she stayed in the hospital for nine months. I vowed to breast-feed my next baby for at least eighteen months. Oh, yes.

Nicole (right) and Nyphen (left) Sanders

So when I had Nyphen (Nypie), I did not hesitate to be as generous with my breast as Nypie possibly wanted, and the kid knew it, too. The little stinker, he refused to even taste the infant milk while breast-feeding. Will anyone blame him? Any child who has tasted the breast milk will not want to drink the infant milk. The taste of the breast milk is indescribable. "You got to taste it to believe it." Unfortunately, Nypie weaned himself after three months due to inconsistency as a result of my job. My consolation was that he had had fun the three months he was breast-fed. I used the nursing brassiere sparingly. I felt it was not natural. I wanted my son to be able to have a feel of the breast, to hold it, to rub it, to drag it, to do whatever he wanted to do with it, no restriction. That is what my mother did, this is what other African women do. To me, a nursing brassiere is restrictive. While in the public, though, I did use the nursing brassiere to please my husband, who even then did not want me to breast-feed in the "open."

I remember on one occasion at the hospital, Nypie was uncomfortable and just wanted a feel of the breast in his mouth, I guess. His father, Ernest, suggested the pacifier, but Nypie spat it out with so much force that I wondered where such a strength came from. Ernest gently picked him up and gave him his milk, but Nypie would not open his mouth. I said to Ernest, "He wants the breast." Ernest replied, "He's gonna have to wait." Just then, as if he understood, Nypie gave a loud holler. Without thinking, I yanked my son away from Ernest, forgot about the nursing brassier, raised my blouse up, and whipped out my breast (as we do in Africa) straight into my son's mouth. Nypie had never sucked so hard. With one suck, I thought my nipple was sore. Ernest, on the hand, was so embarrassed that he not only covered my breast with Nypie's blanket, he shielded us with his body and whispered into my ear, "Not in front of everybody. You could be sued for sexual harassment."

That singular statement of his made me so worked up that I wanted to shout, "Hey everybody, look, I am breast-feeding my baby, you wanna sue me?" But in Africa, when you are breast-feeding, you do not get mad, you do not cry, you avoid all negative experience or turn such experiences into the positive to avoid the ancestors turning your child into a pessimistic and unambitious individual because you have broken the rule; for it is believed that whatever emotions you have are passed on to the baby during breast-feeding and that you cannot hide your emotions from the ancestors, who want you to pass on only positive emotions. If, however, you cannot control your negative emotions, then you must stop breast-feeding temporarily. As it turned out, I was able to control my emotions. But after nursing Nypie, I said to Ernest, "I cannot understand you Americans. Why someone would sue me for sexual harassment for breast-feeding my own baby, I do not know. After all, I did not offer him my breast, neither did I compel him to look at me. If this is what they call 'civilization' then I am afraid I am not civilized."

Breast milk is the African baby's first food. The people,

therefore, cannot understand why a wife would not breast-feed her baby, even if she is from a foreign culture. Such a wife will not be trusted. She has started on the wrong side, and she will make for herself a lot of enemies. "Why will a mother not breast-feed?" asked Agogomeje, an accountant with a prominent bank in Nigeria. "Probably because she doesn't want her breast to drop," answered his colleague, Yesufu. "Nonsense," said Agogomeje, "the breast will drop anyway with the pregnancy hormones," he concluded. "If my wife refuses to breast-feed my baby, then she will go back to her father's house," Okekenebe (the bank manager) echoed, without invitation, looking all stern and mean.

Chapter Four

Being Single

Although things are beginning to change, single parenting is still highly frowned upon. The single mother is considered a disgrace and a letdown to her parents, who feel that they have failed. A single woman is not respected, no matter how educated she is or how highly placed she is career-wise. Landlords do not trust her enough to rent her a home. Amoge, a midwife at a very reputable hospital, told how she had to use her younger brother to pose as her husband in other to get a place to rent. Because her brother did not live with her, they had to fabricate that he was a sailor, on the seas most of the time, just to avoid suspicion. Says Amoge, "I just got tired of being turned down. A fellow spinster gave me this idea and it worked." I could relate to Amoge's experience. After college, even though I had a good paying job, was ready to pay the one-year asking price for rent, it took me fifteen months before I was able to get a place to rent. One landlord, a Christian, turned me down because he was afraid that I would fornicate, and if I did, the sins would be upon his head for renting me a home.

A single woman living with a man is considered "loose," undisciplined. The single woman faces a lot of humiliation. Any man, whether married or single, could grab her "bottom" or breast and boast about the texture, whether soft or firm, to his peers. There is no such thing as sexual harassment. The single woman is considered "not settled." She is referred to as "everyone's wife." She is called names: "prostitute," "hooker," "rocker," "generous donor," among others. It is assumed that any man can sleep with her. Anywhere she turns, she is asked, "When are you getting married?" "Why are you not married?" "What are you waiting for?" "Why are you so choosy?"

The single female faces a lot of pressure from her mother, aunts, married friends and even from her brothers, who constantly remind her to look for a man to take care of her, even if she is independent. This pressure becomes excessively unbearable when most of her friends get married before her. Her mother is mocked and branded a witch! Her mother is asked, "What are you still doing with this big girl in your house?" even though everyone knows that she no longer lives with her parents. Here, when a woman hits thirty years old and beyond, it is automatically assumed that her biological "clock" has expired, that she will no longer be able to bear children. This pressure and the fear of not being able to bear children compels educated and career single females to become the second, third, fourth or fifth wife, a situation they had previously criticized when younger.

A thirty-something female dating a thirty-something male is considered lucky or fortunate to find her age-mate. This age-mate of hers expects her to worship him, to be subservient to him, even if he does not have a job or a home of his own. He constantly reminds his girl-friend how "hot" he is and how other females are ready to "snatch" him away from her if she does not respond to his "beck and call." The female in turn caters to his whims and caprices for fear that she may never find her age-mate to marry again. In actuality, she considers herself fortunate, because her female counterparts are either third wives or are chronically single without a boyfriend. In most cases, these age-mates use these women as a stepping stone to get started in life, then dump them with never-ending excuses ranging from "too old," "does not get along with my mother," to "not able to bear children," even if he had been the one encouraging her not to be pregnant until they get married.

Dada and Damashekpegbe (Dama) knew each other for eighteen years and dated ten years before getting married. Dada had been fortunate to get a scholarship from an oil company to go to London for her master's degree two years after teaching with her bachelor's degree. Dada returned (with the best-looking sports car) to a good job and a big, highly furnished and well-decorated house. Upon Dada's return, Dama could not wait to marry her. He had no job. "He wants to use you," screamed Dada's mother, Iyidada. But Dada would not listen. She was in love. "Why didn't he marry you all these years?" asked Iyidada. "We were students," Dada answered.

Dama refused to perform the traditional Native Law and Customs and instead wedded Dada in court, "because we will have a marriage certificate to prove it," he said. Dada's parents were livid with anger, Dada's mother, especially. She told Dada that Dama's taking her to court was a way of avoiding marrying her, because in his parents' "eye" and in the "eye" of the community, Dama was not married. Dada replied, "Oh, this is the '90s."

After the court marriage, Dama moved in with Dada. He encouraged her not to become pregnant because he was still finding his "feet." In his words, "I don't want my children to rely on a woman's salary." Even though he knew that Dada worked in an established oil company, making good money, he was excessively controlling and manipulative. He would not let Dada go anywhere and was very jealous of Dada's friends. Dada did everything he said because she did not want to appear arrogant, being the bread-winner of the family.

Dada's friends nicknamed her "twitty." Dama drove Dada's car, while she took a cab, even to visit her parents. "What a fool you are, using a cab while a man drives your car!" cried her mother. "He's a man, Mama," replied

Dada. Iyidada shook her head. "I pray for you, my daughter," she said. Dama was always complaining, "Oh, I have no job. How can I be depending on a woman!" He kept a daily log of the mileage of the car, so even if Dada took the car for grocery shopping, he complained, "Oh, because it's your car." If the car did not start, it was because Dada drove it. Dama would scream, "I told you not to drive this car. You don't know how to drive!" Dama was practically complaining about everything. Each year he would say to Dada, "Next year, when my business picks up, we will begin a family." When that year came, he would say, "Oh, I am not ready yet." "Have your children," implored Dada's mother. "Don't wait until he is ready. He may never be ready." Dada replied, "No, you taught me not to disobey my husband, remember?" Dama's complaints became unbearable when, after seven years, the car went "dead," kaput. Dama said, "No car, no work, no business, nothing. What am I suppose to do now?"

Dama had a bachelor's degree in education, but he refused to teach. He called a teacher's salary "peanuts." Dada's aunt, Aletorogidigbo (Alegidi), who was their next-door neighbor and who had "strong connection" in the right places, got tired of Dama's complaints and introduced him to one of her friends, a big shot in an oil company, who then gave Dama a big contract with big money to go with it. As soon as Dama received a partial payment of the money, he bought a Mercedes-Benz.

According to Dada, "He became more loving than ever, no more complaints. I became the perfect wife, or so I thought. He was so good. He would let me drive his car, he no longer kept mileage logs, he encouraged my friends to come over. Everyone was happy for me. I became the envy of my friends and neighbors. Part of his contract was to decorate homes for oil workers, and he got me involved buying and sewing curtains, blinds, picking and hanging paintings and pictures, and so on. Even my mama was beginning to trust him. We were so happy that he now wanted to start a family. Friends said to me, 'Oh, your patience has paid off.' I was overjoyed. I could not thank Aunt Alegidi enough. Then, all of a sudden, one day, without warning, no hint of any kind, I returned home from work to find our home in total disarray. Everything was scattered and out of place. I screamed, *Ole jirunmi dede ren oooh* ('I have been robbed'). I didn't know what to do. But I soon noticed that only my husband's properties were missing. I became apprehensive. 'Oh God! My husband has been kidnapped!' I thought. I knew he was to get the final contract payment that day. 'Who has Dama told about this?' I pondered. 'Oh, God, please help me,' I prayed. I panicked. I took a cab to his parents, crying all the way. 'What will I tell them?' I wondered. To my greatest surprise, as soon as I arrived, his younger brother announced, 'She has come.' 'Were they expecting me or what?' I mused. His mama walked towards me. She was very serious. 'Oh, my, she has heard I'm in trouble.' I cried, 'Mama, Mama, I can't find my husband.' She replied, "Your husband, my son, is not married. You took him to court, you married him, he did not marry you. Thank God the scale you put in his eyes has fallen off at last. All my life, I have never seen where a man will move in with a woman. Your voodoo has gone back to you. My son now has his own place.' His mama went on and on. I just stood there, mystified. I went to his Aunt Oburu, a secretary. She said, 'Please, leave my nephew alone. He never loved you in the first place.' I was flabbergasted. I thought Aunt Oburu and I had an understanding; we got along fine, or so I thought."

Dada continued: "It took me three weeks to locate Dama's place. He was living in one of the homes I had decorated. When I finally caught up with him, he would not talk to me, neither would he let me into his house. He met me by the door. 'What happened, Dama? What happened? Please tell me!' I begged. But Dama said nothing. 'Please come home,' I pleaded. He responded, 'Home, which home? a woman's home? Dada, I never had a home. I was squatting. Please go.' He shut the door. At this point, I heard a woman laughing, and I saw her peeping through the window to look at me. But I wouldn't give up that easily. I went to the head of his extended family, Chief Isoko. Chief said, 'If a man does not want a woman, there is nothing we can do. If you were married, we would have intervened, but you were lovers.' 'Lovers?' I could not believe my ears. Chief continued, 'All my life, I have never heard of a woman who does not want to have children, never! Dada, you are the first one.' Without waiting for me to respond, Chief showed me the door. I could not believe what I just heard. '*Oluwa mi!* (my God) is this what Dama told his people, that I did not want to have children?' I asked myself. I cried to my mother. Mama said, 'Do not worry, my daughter, we learn every day. The Lord shall bring your man.' 'My man?' I screamed. 'Eighteen years, Mama, eighteen years, all wasted. Look at me, thirty-something, closer to forty. All my youth I spent with him. I gave him everything. I denied myself a lot of life pleasures just to make him comfortable, and what did I get in return?' Mama cried as she listened. I expected her to say, 'I told you so,' but she didn't. Like me, she just cried and cried. In reminiscence, Dama never cared. He just used me to get started. How could I have been so blind. How?" Dada stopped and stared into the heavens.

In some cases, these women, anxious to get married, become pregnant, but these men will use this as an excuse to dump them. They call this stubbornness or dis-obedience. "A disobedient girlfriend," the men say, "will make a disobedient wife."

Primarila (Prima') and Emma were college sweethearts. Emma came from a humble family, "street" smart; Prima' from a middle-class family, "book" smart and gullible. All through the four years they spent in college, Prima' cooked for Emma, served him as only a wife or a mother would. She manually washed and ironed his clothes. She took care of his expenses from her pocket money. Only close friends of Primarila knew her first name; the majority of students knew her as "Mrs.

Emma." Emma even referred to her as "my wife." It was only natural for Prima' to assume that Emma would marry her, especially after he had introduced himself to her parents, who paid for all of his summer vacation with their daughter overseas. Emma had always said he could not wait to be a father. He always boasted that he would be the first to be a father amongst his bachelor class-mates. During the last vacation he and Prima' took, they spent a lot of money buying things for their wedding. During the last semester of their final year, when Prima' told him that she was missing her period, Emma said, "Go look for it." According to Prima', she thought it was a joke, but she soon realized that Emma meant it when he started avoiding her and was seen openly in the company of other women. He claimed that Prima' did not ask for his "permission" to get pregnant.

Prima' was distraught; she didn't know what to do. She was too scared to tell her father for fear of being reject-ed. She was even more scared to think of abortion for fear of "heavenly" punishment. She summed up courage and told her mother. Her mother advised Prima' to go back to school, to prepare for her exams and that she, the mother, would take care of Emma. Prima' went back to school. The next day, in the morning, there was a heavy commotion in the males' hostel. Students were running helter-skelter, screaming for help. Prima' looked out the window and behold, in the front of these students, was Emma, with her father in tow, holding a very big *koboko* cane and running like an Olympian, saying something Prima' could not hear. After this episode, Emma came back to Prima, with apologies. He said he was merely trying to see how much love Prima' had for him. They eventually got married. Prima's father was not only a big shot, but a rascal who believes in "jungle" justice. What if this had happened to someone else?

Chapter Five

Wife's Expectations

The African woman's lifestyle is very simple, unpretentious, humble and unassuming. She is gullible, very trusting and trustworthy. She is taught not to look directly into the eyes of a man, in order to avoid adultery. She is expected to marry and stay married and bear many children, to accept any and all illegitimate children without question and bring them up as her own. "Why should an innocent child suffer? Is it the fault of the child to be born? Who knows tomorrow? Who knows the child that will 'bury' one?" the local folks will ask. The African woman is exposed to these questions early in life. She is taught that children are "Spirits." "If you are kind to a child today, you will reap the reward tomorrow, though not necessarily from the child that you were kind to." She is expected to make the best of an unhappy marriage because of the children. Parents will say to their daughters, " If you leave, your children will suffer. No one will take care of your children as well as you. Your presence alone, means a lot. Stay put!" The locals will ask, "Why would a woman with children be unhappy, anyway? She has the children to keep her company, to keep her busy."

The wife is expected to perfect the act of cooking. Cooking is a big deal. It is said that "the fastest way to a man's heart is through his stomach." A daughter who does not know how to cook, it is believed, is a reflection of her mother, and this is a disgrace. Her mother becomes a joke and a laughing stock. This is very shameful indeed. The other wives make jest of mother and daughter, and this spreads like wildfire. On the other hand, if a woman is a good cook, that word spreads too, and all praises go to her mother. This reflects on all the females in the extended family and on generation upon generation after her. Males are referred to that family to pick a wife because "the women are very good cooks."

Female smoking is slightly tolerated in the Northern part of the country, because at certain times of the year (harmattan season) it is colder in that part of the country than any other part. In the South, it is an abomination for a woman to smoke. Female smokers are called names: *ashawo*, "prostitute," "hooker," *kobokobo, igber-*

aja; the names are endless. So if a man introduces a "smoker" wife to his people, even if she is a foreigner, the people, wide-eyed, will say to one another (sotto voce), "She smokes." This means the wife has no proper upbringing. Such a woman is considered "loose," not to be trusted. Without knowing who she is, she is disliked already. Such a wife can never please the natives, no matter how hard she tries. Sometimes, husbands try to protect such wives by asking them not to smoke in the presence of the natives, but some women will not listen; they say, "I want to be myself." As Ernest would say, "Good luck, baby."

A wife is expected to be dignified. A dignified woman is one who can keep secrets, who listens quietly and talks less, who is patient, tolerant, accommodating, compliant and does as she is told. A woman is expected to stay married forever. When a marriage collapses, it is the woman's fault; when a marriage is together, the man is in control.

A wife is also expected to control her sexual libido, to report to her husband if any man looks at or winks at or smiles excessively at her. Shaking a man's hand in the Urhobo Delta culture, and in some other cultures, is considered adultery; therefore, the wife must confess so that the ancestors will be appeased on her behalf. Rather than shaking a man's hand, if a man offers a handshake, the wife responds with her elbow. A wife is not expected to see the nakedness of any man. If, however, her profession, such as the medical profession, encourages her to be so exposed, she is obligated to tell the husband of each exposure and to honestly and truthfully answer any and all the questions the husband asks. Such questions include and are not limited to: "Were you turned on when you saw his penis?" "Was it big or small?" "Was it straight or crooked?" "Any distinguishing marks?" Any sign of hesitation or expression of anger from the wife is considered adultery, and the ancestors must be appeased before the husband can have any sexual intimacy with her. However, because of the laws protecting women abroad, the African husband cannot directly ask his foreign wife in the medical field these questions, and this breeds unnecessary tension within the family. The husband gets mad unnecessarily either when the wife is going to work or when she returns from work. The unsuspecting wife does not know where this anger is coming from.

A wife is expected to understand that it is un-African for a man to express outward emotion or to apologize. The African man does not say, " I am sorry." This is unmanly and shows weakness and lack of control. His actions will show how sorry he is. In domestic or matrimonial disagreements, the wife is expected to request the husband's extended family members' intervention or, where the family is not available, the husband's best friends, but not the police. It is sinful and insulting to call the police for one's husband. It shows disrespect and a lack of control in the family. It is a shame on the woman. In Nigeria, if a woman calls the police for her husband, the police will not come; they will laugh and ridicule her. They will say to her, "What kind of wife are you? Stupid woman, are you the only one having trouble with your husband? Look at her mouth, big mouth. You should be ashamed of yourself. Run out of my sight before I kick your *yansh* (ass)." Calling the police leads to reject and isolation. Going to jail is a stigma, a shame, a disgrace.

There is no such thing as domestic abuse. A husband can do to his wife and children as he pleases. In some cultures, hot pepper is put into the eyes and private parts of a stubborn daughter. Children are beaten up with big sticks, slippers, or brooms by their parents without intervention of any kind. The impression is that the parents brought them into this world, if they want to kill them, so be it. This is called "discipline." Evelyn, a school teacher, agreed that sometimes parents go too far in the name of discipline, but that some of these children really need a tough hand. Felicia, a school principal, said that she does not believe in being flogged, but concluded that if her parents had not been tough with her, she would not be where she is today. Felicia did not define "toughness."

Even though it is a sin to call the police in matrimonial disagreements, each community has a way of checking husbands. In the Delta area, for instance, husbands are checked by the oldest women in the community, the *Egweya*. To be eligible to be a member of this Egweya group, you have to have a good reputation and be born at a certain period that will qualify you to be at least 70 years old and above. One does not apply to be a member of this group; when the time comes, the group will contact you. This is the most respected group that fights for a woman's cause in this area. Husbands dread incurring their wrath. When a woman comes to report to this group that her husband is "mean" to her, to his children, or to all of his wives, these old women will investigate.

If the Egweya find the husband guilty, the old women will gather together, go to the husband's compound in the "wee hours" of the morning, completely naked. In front of his compound, they will call his name three times and say, "We, the oldest women group, have heard how mean you are to your family. We have come to open our *toto* (vagina) for you." Then they will begin to sing with the man's name, telling all the mean things he does. They will conclude with, "It is through this toto (all the naked women pointing to the vagina) that you were formed. It is through this toto that you came into this world, and it is this toto that will kill you." The women, still completely naked, will start dancing and clapping their hands, slapping their butts, singing loudly, until they get to the man's doorstep. At the doorstep, they all in one swift move will bend and show the man their butts. Passers-by dare not look, for it is believed that looking at these women will bring bad luck to the onlooker. Most husbands are too embarrassed to look into a group of old women's naked butts, so they shy away. This is a warning.

Most of the time, this is enough to turn a mean husband around. This is a shame indeed to such a husband who will be laughed to scorn by his peers. He will have no place to hide his face. He becomes a laughing stock to the whole community, a joke. Husbands have been known to flee from a community, never to return after such an encounter. It is said that the fastest way to get the ancestors to act is through this group, for they (the ancestors) do not take it lightly when these women open their "toto." The ancestors become real "mean" and mad with such a husband.

However, if the husband is stubborn and continues to be mean, the oldest women, naked, singing and dancing before him, will invoke the spirit of the ancestors and curse him. It is believed that the "toto" is a very powerful "weapon," that it can make and unmake a man, that if a man hurts a woman and she uses her "toto" to "swear" or curse the man, such a curse is irreversible. Prostitutes cheated or defrauded by men have been known to use this method to gain justice.

Chapter Six

Husbands

Who is the Nigerian man? He is very charming and charismatic, flamboyant and ostentatious. He carries himself well, always conscious of his looks. He dresses to match at all times. He loves expensive wristwatches, expensive colognes, and expensive cars. He drives the best of cars, Mercedes, Lamborgine, BMW (the men call it "Be My Wife"), S.U.V.s, Rolls Royce, all sorts of luxury cars. You can't help but notice a Nigerian man. Previously, one could stand on the street in Nigeria and be admiring cars all day but today, these cars are overshadowed by smokey vehicles polluting the air; and nothing is being done about air pollution. These cars are all paid for. Here, if you don't have the cash, you don't buy, you don't build. Credit cards are only for the privileged few. The average Nigerian carries a lot of cash on him/her. It is the people's culture. The man likes qualitative quantity; that is, he buys quality in abundance. In his mind, the more expensive, the better the quality.

The more a woman plays hard to get, the more the man appreciates her. He likes to be the "chaser." He loves and enjoys such challenges; it doesn't matter how long it takes. He says to his peers, "*I go getam*" (I will conquer). He stoops to conquer. He has an insatiable need to "conquer." After "conquering," the excitement dissipates.

He is very generous. He prefers giving money to buying flowers. When he takes a woman out, he pays all the bills. He feels insulted if the woman offers to pay. This is the Nigerian way. When two friends or more go out together, one person takes the initiative to pay for everyone, expecting nothing in return. Here, when a party is held, it is free food and drinks (all sorts of drinks) for all. There is nothing like BYOB (bring your own bottle). The Nigerian party ends at dawn. There is no starting time. Even though the invitation card may say, "Party starts at 8 p.m.," guests do not arrive at the party until about 10 p.m. This is called "African time." The party host/hostess has the option of discouraging "African Time" by emphasizing in the invitation card, "Please, no African Time."

The man wants his woman to look good at all times. He buys her the best of clothes, the best of shoes, the best of everything. He has a way with words. He is slick, smooth, persuasive, and convincing. Women love him. He loves women, too. He will look you straight in the eye and tell you what you want to hear. He has a way of making every woman he meets feel special and loved. He is a great flatterer. In his mind, he knows he is saying things he does not mean, but he says it anyway. Just as he makes one woman feel special, so he makes the other. But wait a minute, is this peculiar to the Nigerian man or is it men in general? Does he mean to hurt or is it because of his culture? What is expected of him, anyway? Deceit is not a part of the Nigerian culture. The culture encourages honesty and patience.

The husband is expected to be strong at all times, to conceal his emotions. Crying is a sign of weakness; it is an embarrassment to his father, who will be seen as even weaker. It is also considered unmanly to sneak behind one's wife to have an affair; the husband was brought up to be as open about his affairs as he possibly can. He was brought up to appreciate beauty and acts of beauty. Big or fat is beautiful; it is a sign of "good living." Thinness is ugly and manly, evidence of suffering. When you say to the Nigerian, "You are losing weight," it's like saying, "You are suffering." He/she becomes defensive. But when you say, "You've gained weight," it's like saying, "You are living well."

The average husband says that he wants to hold some meat, not bones. In the Eastern part of the country, there is a place called "the fattening room," where new brides are sent to be fed "fat," so as to look "womanly" for their husbands. He says he appreciates *ikebe supper*, that is, a "very big bottom," rolling from side to side, with no girdle. He appreciates very big breasts, too. "The bigger the boobs," he says, "the more milk for my children." A big stomach is synonymous with fertility. It is assumed that a thin person with a flat stomach and thin hips will not be able to carry a pregnancy or deliver a child. The advent of television and the influence of foreign culture is beginning to change some men's perception. However, others remain adamant on preferring fat women. Says Haruna, "Because of the emphasis of 'strong body' or muscles or whatever they call it, that is why people cannot differentiate between men and women today." He continued, "A woman should be succulent, supple and soft, not hard." Different Africans have different opinions on this subject. Some prefer thinness, while a majority prefer "flesh." On the whole, the husband is expected to acquire and "own" desirable women.

Displaying affection or putting on earrings, whether in one or both ears, is associated with feminism, weakness. If a husband so much as displays open affection for his wife, he is labeled as "woman wrapper," meaning that the wife ties him around her waist, just as she ties her traditional wrapper attire. In other words, "She's got his number"; she is in control. Such a man is mocked, made fun of, not respected, and the whole community makes jest of his parents and siblings alike. No one wants to give a wife to such a man because he is weak, lacks control, and cannot defend his family. "What kind of man is this?" the folks will ask. Even his mother will question the ancestors, "What did I do to deserve such a *mumu* (foolish) son?"

A husband is not expected to experience morning sickness during his wife's pregnancy. When I visited home, family members anxious to hear about my new husband asked a lot of questions, amongst which was, "Patience, how did he treat you when you were pregnant?" "Oh, he was wonderful," I answered, then continued, "I craved corn on the cob and ice cream a lot. He would get out of bed even at one in the morning to prepare it for me." At this point my uncles started fidgeting on their seats. They looked at each other in disbelief. But my aunts wanted to hear more. They asked. "How were you able to keep ice cream down without throwing up?" I replied, "I was never sick one day. No symptoms of any kind. I just carried the baby; my husband was the sick one. He was sicker than a dog. He could not keep down food for the first trimester. Even the smell of perfume would induce vomit. He was very weak and tired. At the hospital, the nurses asked him how he felt and gave him crackers to eat to prevent vomiting. At work, they were very sympathetic. They encouraged him to take time off and gave him water to wash his face after each vomit."

As I was speaking, my uncles were shaking their heads from side to side in disbelief. As I opened my purse to bring out a picture of my husband braiding our daughter's hair, one of my uncles said, "You didn't mean what you just said about your husband having morning sickness, did you?" "Yes, sir, I did." (His expression made me put the picture back in my purse immediately.) Uncle exclaimed, "Wonders shall never end! How can a man experience morning sickness? He was not the one carrying the baby, so where did the morning sickness come from?" One of my aunts replied, "It is love. He was empathizing with his wife." Uncle turned to her and, pointing his right index finger, he asked, "Did your father have morning sickness? Did your own husband have morning sickness? Are you telling me he doesn't love you? Where in the whole wide world have you heard that a man suffers from morning sickness?"

Turning to me, Uncle said, "And you, Patience, an African woman, instead of you telling the man to stop that nonsense, you didn't, you started telling us. Are you not ashamed?" He continued, "I do not know who is more stupid, whether it is the man who was having morning sickness or the nurses at the hospital that offered him crackers to eat." Uncle wasn't done yet. Turning to his sisters, he said, "You people call it love? Which of you here will want her son to experience morning sickness?" All the women looked away. Turning to me, he asked, "Will you want *Nyny* to experience morning sickness?" "His name is pronounced Nyfen, Uncle," I corrected. "Answer me," he growled. "Uncle," I answered, "I have no control over this. My husband's father experienced morning sickness too. It is normal for a man to have morning sickness. When a woman is pregnant, the man is also pregnant. The symptoms could manifest either in the woman or the man. It doesn't make the man any less of a man." Uncle said, "Is that what they told you in America? You haven't answered my question. How will you, an African woman, feel if your son says he is experiencing morning sickness?" I answered, "Uncle, I will like to be like my mother-in-law, very sympathetic and understanding, always calling to check on her son, giving him recipes of food to prevent vomit, making sure he has enough rest and not keeping him on the phone for too long."

Uncle listened, shook his head, and said, "I will tell you one thing I know for a fact, *Nyny* will not have morning sickness." Uncle paused for a few seconds, kept his head down as if in deep thoughts. Suddenly he raised his head and asked me, "You know why that kid will never have such a senseless experience? Because he has a Nigerian blood in him." Speaking through clenched teeth, Uncle said, "Now, when you get back, tell that man that I, your uncle, said that I do not want to hear that he ever experienced morning sickness again." Walking away, seething, right fist clenched, Uncle muttered, "Morning sickness, my foot!" This is the way the average Nigerian thinks about morning sickness. A man bold enough to acknowledge morning sickness will be laughed to scorn. He will be made to feel less of a man.

One thing the husband is not expected to do is to beat his wife. This is considered belittling oneself, humiliating. Rather than beat his wife, the African man will not eat her food. This is considered a rejection, and rejection is a shame indeed. Not only will he not eat her food, he will not ask her for simple favors nor will he let her do anything for him, such as drawing his water or massaging his back or removing gray hairs (if any) from his head or from any other sites. When she greets him, he acknowledges her with a simple nod of his head. She becomes the laughing stock of the whole household and the community. It does not matter if she was right or wrong. The word spreads like breeze that so-and-so has been rejected by her husband. He will not send the wife away, but she becomes very uncomfortable. She is free to move out, but where will she go? If she goes to her parents, what will she say? Her discomfort is especially compounded by other family members, including some of the wives and children, taking sides with the husband, therefore isolating the reject. To rectify this, the wife rallies around the male members of the husband's family to appease him on her behalf, a situation that may involve one of several penalties, maybe a huge fine, buying a "drink," or maybe being barred from sleeping with the husband for any length of time, up to three years. (However, there have been occasions where women barred up to three years have become pregnant in less than a year.)

In Africa, when a husband beats his wife he hits her very gently. He does not fight her the way he would fight a fellow man. A husband who beats his wife, however, faces the wrath of the male members of the wife's family. Her father, her brothers, her cousins and nephews will beat the husband to stupor and warn him never to touch their "sister" again. For this reason, a wife beaten by her husband in most cases is afraid to tell her family; she may confide in her mother, woman to woman, and hope that she will not tell. In most cases, the mother, non-judgmental, will only tell if the daughter's life is in danger. One would have expected a wife to seek "revenge" by telling her family, but no, not the African woman. She is very accommodating and full of compassion.

The African woman is extremely patient. She may appear docile, but she is not. As a young girl, if there was anything I criticized my mother for, it was her patience. I would say to her, "Mama, you are too patient. People may misconstrue your patience for foolishness." Mama would respond, "My daughter, it takes a wise person to act foolishly, but a foolish person can never act wisely. *Patience doesn't hurt.*" Mama would conclude with, "I know what I am doing."

The African woman is very observant but does not complain about everything she sees. But God help the husband when she runs out of patience. Her mouth is her weapon. She will talk without stopping. She will revisit past experiences, reiterate all the things he has done for years. If he says, "But I thought you forgave me; why are you bringing it up again?" she will respond, "Forgiven but not forgotten. The past determines the future. You did it before, you will do it again, but don't you think I will take it from you this time." Believe me, don't get her mad, because when the African woman makes up her mind, she doesn't "look back." Children are careful not to overstep their boundaries because the mother's "talk" would drive them crazy. Children may say to their mothers, "I would rather you beat me and get it over with. Your 'talk' would make me go out of my mind." To this the mother would respond, "You haven't heard anything yet." Husbands are careful not to intervene at this time. The wise husband walks away. If he so much as says to the wife, "That's enough," the wife will turn on him and say, "Why am I not surprised at his behavior? Like father like child." Then she would "descend" on the man with a vengeance telling him all the things he thought she had not noticed. If he asks, "Why didn't you tell me before now?" she would respond, "Because I wanted to give you a long rope to hang yourself, and indeed you just did."

Not only will she continue to talk, she will not sleep with her husband when she is angry. The men call this behavior "punishment." If the man says, "I will report you to your father," she will respond, "Go ahead, report me." In most cases, however, husbands are afraid to report this because the African father is extremely protective of his daughter. The African woman is believed to be very obedient and patient; if, therefore, she refuses to sleep with her husband, the father believes that she is justified. If the husband *does* report her to her father, the father will respond that "her thing" belongs to her and that she can do whatever she likes with "it" as long as she does not commit adultery. If the husband says to the wife, "I will go get 'it' from other women," she will respond, "Will this be the first time? Go sleep with Queen Elizabeth if you like, I don't care. But this *toto*"—pointing to her vagina—"you no go get!" And the husband will *not* get "it" as long as his wife is angry. The African woman guards and cherishes her most important weapon—her vagina.

But the African husband understands his wife. He knows how to pacify her. He will not get mad at her at this time, trying to curry favor, going out of his way to do things which under normal circumstances he would not do.

The African husband expects his wife to be quiet when he is talking. If she so much as opens her mouth to speak while he is talking, shouting at the top of his voice, he says, "I am talking," implying that the wife was being rude by talking without being told to do so. He expects his wife to leave the room whenever he is in a discussion with any member of his family, unless he asks her to stay. If the husband does not tell his wife to leave, his family member has the right to do so, and the husband dares not stop the family member: the reason being that a wife is not supposed to know what goes on in the husband's family. Knowing breeds "chick," insult and eventually disrespect to the husband. The husband's family, there-fore, is merely protecting what is "theirs."

Because of the unstated acceptable definition of gender roles in the African culture, most foreign wives I have come in contact with find it very difficult to understand the culture. They ask their husbands a lot of questions, which, in the culture, is considered stubbornness, a threat to his manhood. When the husband feels threat-ened and intimidated by his foreign wife, he may look for and marry a woman he feels comfortable with, in most cases, an African woman in his homeland. He may or may not tell his "foreign" wife, especially since the African wife will live in Africa. He phones his African wife frequently, sends her money and presents regularly. The African wife is content living in Africa. He makes her comfortable, builds her a home, buys her a car, sets her up in some business, and goes home to visit her (on a prolonged visit) once or twice a year. His friends may know but say nothing to his foreign wife, because in this community the African wife is regarded as his "real wife," respected and revered; his foreign wife is seen as a foreigner without culture.

In Nigeria, if the husband's brother pays a visit, the wife is expected to leave their bedroom for the brother-in-law, unless told otherwise. The brothers share the same bed. If the sister-in-law visits, however, she is given the guest room to stay. It is insulting to ask the husband's relative how long he/she is going to stay. The house belongs to the brother, and the in-law can stay as long as he/she wishes. Here, two men or two women will share the same bed without raising eyebrows. If a female friend visits another female friend, or if a male friend visits another male friend, they will share the same bed and talk all night long, "catching up." They will hug innocently.

Isaiah, for example, lived in America for six years before visiting home. His best friend, Santana, heard of his visit and came rushing, giving him a big bear hug. According to Isaiah, "I stiffened. Santana asked, 'Are you all right?' At bedtime, Santana jumped into the bed with me, talking and talking and talking. He just could not hear enough of America. Finally he fell asleep, but I was so restless that Santana said, 'Isaiah, why are you so restless? You better quit moving up and down like a worm and let me sleep.' This was when I realized that I was home."

Sisters dress and undress before their brothers without problems. Mothers dress and undress before their husbands, sons, and nephews without problems. No one says anything. Sometimes the brothers or uncle or nephews even help to hook up the brassieres. It is normal. The men show no lust, no enthusiasm towards these women. Incest is an abomination. During the writing of this book, there was a Registered Nurse, an African American married to a Kenyan in Minnesota who was concerned about the husband's eighteen-year-old sister sharing the same bed with her husband. According to the foreigner, her husband told her that this was the practice in Africa. This foreigner wanted to know from my friend, Josephine, who is from Sierra Leone, if her husband was right. This is not the practice. Josephine's response couldn't have been more appropriate. She said, "Whether from West Africa or East Africa, or from any part of Africa, any eighteen-year-old female who shares the same bed with your husband wants to take your husband from you." Josephine asked, "Patience, what is wrong with our African brothers?" When my friend

Linda heard, she was very distraught. She asked, "Why do these African men represent us so poorly?" Please note that there is no part in the whole of the African continent where mature brothers and sisters or cousins or any type of relative of the opposite sex share the same bed. As the old African adage goes, "When a man is erect, he knows not his mother."

Chapter Seven

Sex

The African wife is very discreet. She is taught to keep a lot of secrets for fear that what she says may be used against her, her children, and generations of women after her. Sex is the most sacred and secretive thing to talk about. In fact, it is a taboo to talk about sex in the open. She is made to believe that sex is for procreation, that it is forbidden for a woman to ask for it from her husband. This belief is embedded into the young girl from childhood. She is told, "You don't get it until he comes to you." Only prostitutes "miss" sex. "What is there to miss?" the women will ask.

A disciplined and a responsible woman does not think of sex. Women are conditioned to be without sex up to and beyond three years at a time. Most of the time, women here, genitals mutilated or not, live up to that expectation. Masturbation is considered a sin. The impression is that even putting your hand inside your genitals to wash is sinful. To wash your genitals, you soak your butt in a bathtub or in an improvised bathtub such as a bucket. The African woman takes a total bath at least twice a day. They believe in cleanliness. When a woman reaches menopause, it is assumed that her sex life is over. "What more does she want to do, that she hasn't done all these years?" her husband will ask.

In polygamous homes, the wives take turns sleeping with their husbands. When it is a woman's turn, she takes a bath early in the evening, rubs powder all over her neck and chest, with perfume sprayed from head to toe. In these homes, everyone knows everyone's turn. However, occasionally, the women fight over turns. When another woman rubs powder all over her body and looks real perky and cute, the wife whose turn it is gets mad, resulting in a fight. Or if the woman whose turn it is waits for the husband in vain and then finds out that he was with so-and-so mate, a fight also breaks out, possibly a physical fight that will require the intervention of the extended family members of all the people involved. When asked what happened, the woman concerned, pointing to the mate, will say, "She took my turn." In such a situation, the husband explains why he shunned the wife. The husband tries to honor the "turns," except when mad at the wife. After the husband's explanation, the shunned wife is fined and asked to apologize to the husband and be "nice." Again, it does not matter if she was right or wrong, she must apologize, otherwise the husband will continue to shun her, and she dares not commit adultery.

Adultery is intolerable. In this country, men "do not" commit adultery, only women. A woman who commits adultery is an automatic outcast. Her mother, her sisters, her daughters, her nieces, and generations of women after her suffer the consequences. They are shamed, "booed" at wherever they go. Men are warned not to marry from such a family, because "adultery runs in the family." The whole family is stigmatized, nicknamed "adultery," and this name stays forever. If a pregnant woman experiences a prolonged labor during childbirth, it is automatically assumed that she has committed adultery at one time or another. She is ordered to *Emuworuruta* (confess her sins) so that the ancestors will be appeased to make delivery faster and safe. During this prolonged labor, she is asked a series of questions, "Did another man look at you or did you flirt with a man without telling your husband?" "Did you sleep with another man?" In the pain and hope of getting this over and done with, some women answer "yes." Such women live with the consequence of adultery forever. Even if they deny it afterwards, no one believes them. It is also believed that if a woman commits adultery, the ancestors will kill one or more of her children in order to punish her.

It is a taboo for a woman to dream of making love. If she does, it will be assumed that she has an "evil spirit husband" that must be exorcised. Different cultures have different ways of performing exorcism. If a woman refuses to be exorcised due to her religious belief or lack of belief in the unseen "spiritual husband," then the human husband must divorce her immediately for fear of being killed by the wife's spiritual husband, who, it is believed, is very imperious and jealous. A single woman twenty-five years old and beyond is assumed to have a "spiritual husband" who "spiritually" prevents her from being married. To get a husband to marry, therefore, the "spiritual husband" must be exorcised.

Although sex is hardly ever talked about, the young girl is subtly conditioned not to make the first move in sex or in a romantic relationship. She is told to let the man make the first move, otherwise "you will be considered cheap." A majority of the African men interviewed here said they prefer to make the first move, and that if a woman approaches them for a relationship, they feel that that is how she will approach other guys; they find it difficult to trust such a woman. "Such a woman," the men say, "is good for a girlfriend but not a wife." The advent of television and the Western culture has revolutionized things a little bit, but it is still considered a disgrace for a woman to meet a man and make love to him the first day they meet. One of the African women interviewed told a story of how her mother attempted suicide because she got pregnant from a man she met only once at a party.

They later got married; she was his fifth wife, her child his seventeenth child.

Females are taught to be conservative, to be able to control their "hormones." "Sex," it is drummed into the young formative girl, "is no food." A woman who outwardly expresses joy and moans and moves excessively during lovemaking is considered "spoilt," "rotten," and a disgrace to her mother. Such a woman is okay to have and keep as a mistress, but not good enough for marriage because she is not disciplined. When the man says to his wife, "I won't bother you today if you don't want me to," the disciplined wife is expected to say, "Thank you, my husband, I really don't want to be bothered." But a wife who says, "Oh, it's no bother," is seen as lacking control and untrustworthy. Such a woman is closely watched and guarded by the community. The husband does not have to say much to the community before they know. All he has to say to one person is "so-and-so likes the 'thing' too much," and the word spreads around. The woman's daughters and sisters become untrustworthy, too. Lovemaking is at a man's discretion.

Africans do not participate in "kinky" sex; that is, the man being dressed like a woman, or the man asking to be tied or flogged, or such odd behaviors. When I brought up the subject of anal sex, all the men interviewed asked a similar question, "Pat, have you lived in a foreign land for too long?" "Have you forgotten your culture?" "Don't you know better than that?" The belief is that if a man participates in anal sex, the ancestors will open up his rectum so wide that he will become incontinent, that is, he will not be able to control his "shit" ever again. This topic was so disgusting to Tony, a former colleague, that he *emesed* (vomited). Holding up his hand, palm facing me as if to restrain me, he said, "Please, tell them Africans do no anal sex, no kinky sex, no sex with dogs or pigs or monkeys or any animal. We only sleep with women, period." All the women interviewed denied having participated in anal sex. I was too scared to ask about same sex relationships. To my knowledge, and from personal observation, none exist. If it does, then it must be kept <u>real</u> secret.

A majority of the wives interviewed said that sex is controlled by the man and that the African man does not believe in safe sex because he thinks his exposure to different kinds of germs has made him immune to venereal diseases. The truth is, every country has germs that are unique to that country. One of the wives claimed that all the African men she knew agree on one thing—that "venereal disease is a foreigner's disease and therefore does not affect Africans." The wives agreed that the "missionary position" (a man must always be on top) is very popular among the men, with little or no caress or variation of "styles." The wives just lay there for fear of being branded "rotten" or "spoilt." Ngozi, a legal secretary, asked, "Do these men know any better? They are just like us women, nobody tells them about sex." Indeed, in a culture where watching a pornographic movie is considered a sin, where no one teaches anyone about sex, where all the young man hears about sex is "a man being on top of a woman," how do you expect him to know about sex? I sometimes wonder. Nwankego, an uncircumcised 38-year-old nurse from Cameroon, married for 22 years, asked, "Is it true that women reach orgasm, or is it just a myth?" She continued, "My husband does 'it' for less than a minute, no romance, no caress, nothing. He just jumps on and off me and that is it." Most of the women interviewed agreed that African men don't ask the women if they are satisfied or if they reached orgasm. All they care about is their own satisfaction. In the words of Akwakor, a Ghanaian pharmacist, "It is wham, bam and off, not even a simple 'thank you.'"

I did talk to a few American men about sex. They appeared to be really caring. The American men want their wives to enjoy sex as much as they do. They romance their wives, caress, make the environment right and enticing. They wait for the women to reach orgasm so that both man and woman experience orgasm simultaneously. At the end, the men pay compliments; they say, "Baby, that was good. I enjoyed it, did you? Do you want more?" If, perchance, the wife delayed orgasm, even though the man has reached orgasm, he will use other of his God-given "body parts" to stimulate the wife to reach orgasm. Bessem, a 33-year-old nursing assistant from Benin Republic, asked, "Is sex enjoyable?"

Do African men ever discuss how their wives feel about sex? No! The wife is treated as a sex "machine." A machine is a mechanical instrument without a voice. Can a woman complain to her husband that she does not enjoy sex? Oh, no!! He will get mad at her and call her names—*Ashawo* (prostitute). This will lead to rejection and distrust. Who can the African woman complain to? No one. Not even to her own family members. How would she approach the subject? "Mum, Dad, I don't enjoy sex with my husband"? "*Oturugbeke!*" the parents will exclaim, wondering what has gotten into their daughter. They will search their hearts to see where they failed in raising her right. Such a woman will be humiliated and belittled. Certain things you just don't say. We, the African women, were not born to enjoy sex, I guess.

Some of the foreign wives I talked with wondered why the men do not get "down" on the women; some called it the "6–9" position, others call it "presidential knee pads" or something like that. These women asked why the men do not protest when the women give them a "blow job." The reason is that, in this culture, "getting down" on a woman is un-African, degrading, and would breed *Orimitan*, that is, contempt. "Why will I put my mouth there?" asked Joseph, a multinational stockbroker. "Jeez, is it food?" he asked. "If she does not get wet, use the Vaseline," says Surulere Zillyblack, a famous journalist. The African man was brought up to believe that a real man does not "play" with the vagina. In his mind, the vagina is the dirtiest part of the woman. Yusly, an engineer who studied in Birmingham, England, told a story of his first "suck" experience: he puked all over. Says Yusly, "The smell stayed with me for days. I just kept looking behind me to see if people were making jest of me. I will never try it again." Ahijo, a cab driver, said, "I wouldn't even know when to suck it, that thing bleeds too much."

To the man, a woman has no right to enjoy sex; enjoying sex breeds prostitution. The man gets scared of a woman who loves and enjoys sex. She is good for a girlfriend but not good enough for a wife. He says to his peers, "Ah, the way she twists her waist is unbelievable. She loves sex too much, she will kill me." Some men believe that too much sex causes premature death. The woman, on the other hand, is taught that "sucking a dick" is a sin that requires an intervention of the ancestors. The thinking is, "How can one use the mouth with which one prays to God to suck a dick . . . God forbid!" Upon hearing that I had my daughter, Nicole, at five months' gestation, one of my aunts said, "You must have offended our ancestors." Looking very concerned and worried, she asked, "Is this American man making you put his prick in your mouth?"

It is also forbidden for a woman having her menstrual period to sleep in the same room with her husband. In some cultures, the woman is not allowed to cook for the husband because she is unclean. Eating her food or sharing the same bed breeds bad luck to the man and causes early impotence. This later practice, however, is declining fast; many women agreed that they cook and share the same bed with their husbands during menstruation, though no intercourse takes place during this period.

Sleeping with a woman during her menstruation is a definite no-no. It not only causes early impotence, it exposes the man to the attack of an "evil spirit," according to the belief. A majority of the men interviewed disagreed with the women about African men not caressing and not participating in a variety of styles. One of them aggressively asked, "Who are these women that you interviewed, anyway?" However, the men say that this is a tale to discredit them, that the average African man makes love just as good, if not better, than any other culture, and that they, the men, are very considerate, taking their partner's satisfaction into consideration. The men agreed, however, that "sucking" is not their thing. Both men and women agreed on one thing: that the average African man is "sizable." One of the wives called it "real big," another went "um-m, um-m," curling up her tongue and licking her lips from side to side. She was a foreigner.

Chapter Eight

Female Genital Mutilation

In the ancient times, there was a very high rate of infant mortality. The gods were consulted as to how to stop these infants from dying. The gods revealed that these deaths were due to the clitoris touching the heads of the newborn babies during birth, and that these deaths would stop only if the clitoris were cut off. Legend has it that, with the clitoris cut off, the death rate dropped dramatically. This story was passed on from one generation to another and up to this day. After the gods "verdict," the clitoris was seen, not only as ugly, but as an evil part of the woman that must be completely cut off. Cutting it off is called "circumcision."

The difference between the male circumcision and the female circumcision is that in the male, the foreskin of the male penis is cut off, in the female, it is the clitoris that is totally removed. The clitoris contains nerve endings that are connected to other parts of the body. To cut off the clitoris, the arms and legs of the individual concerned are spread, each arm and leg held down by at least two strong male adults. The clitoris is stimulated, and as the clitoris responds to the stimulation, they cut it off. This is a very painful experience indeed, beyond description. A majority of times, circumcision, whether of the female or the male, is done by crude methods, performed without sterilization, no anesthetics and by untrained persons. No pain-killers are given after the procedure. This in most cases leads to very serious life-threatening infections. People have died after circumcision, but these deaths were believed to be caused by "voodoo" attributed to jealousy of other wives or friends or relatives. Female circumcision could lead to uncontrollable bleeding and infections of the uterus (womb) that could make a woman unable to produce children. But in this culture, sterility is believed to be either punishment from God for one's past deeds or caused again by voodoo.

The age of circumcision varies from culture to culture. In some cultures, it is done during infancy, eight days after the baby is born, or during pregnancy; in other cultures, it is done during adolescence. Circumcision during adolescence is a very beautiful ceremony. The teenager is treated like a queen. She walks on special cloth made of velvety material, specially tailored for this occasion. Her feet do not touch the bare floor. Her room is specially decorated, well lighted. She is dressed in a special regalia for seven days, and for these seven days, she does no household chores. Seven days without household chores for the African female is like going on a one year-paid vacation for "Westerners." For these seven days, her friends are with her, the whole community brings her presents, and she chooses from a variety of specially pre-pared menus. She gets excessive attention from all and sundry. If betrothed, her bride price is paid during this period. If a single teenager, she gets proposed to at this time. Many young girls want to be circumcised because of the beautiful ceremony and the attention that goes with it, unaware of the consequences and the implica-tion.

However, not all cultures in Africa circumcise their females. The Itsekiri tribe, because of their early expo-sure to the Western culture, were told of the importance of the clitoris and were convinced that the clitoris is not the cause of infant mortality. The Itsekiris then stopped circumcising their females, but the Itsekiri female does not believe in giving birth to many children, and the divorce rate among the Itsekiris is very high. This led the Itsekiri neighbors, the Urhobos, a different tribe, who believe in having many children, to believe that the cli-toris not only causes a high infant mortality rate, but also causes divorce and prevents women from giving birth to many children. This latter part was very scary to women of other cultures, especially in a culture where having children is "everything."

A few women think that female genital mutilation should be encouraged to prevent promiscuity. Ubah, a twenty-year-old Somalian studying computer science, said, "Look at the world today. Even twelve-year-old girls have given birth to children. This is wrong. At my age, I am still a virgin, and there are virgins older than me in my country, with no urge for sex. You know why, because our genitals were cut off." When reminded that she may not enjoy sex when she gets married, Ubah replied, "I will not know the difference. Marriage is more than sex," she concluded. Indeed, in Africa today (genital mutilated or not), there are real virgins, not secondary virgins, pure virgins who have neither experienced sexual intercourse nor oral sex even at the age of thirty. Some of them are career women determined to keep themselves for "Mr. Right." But the pressure and fear of not being able to bear children soon gets to them, and they fall prey to men who take advantage of their virginity and boast about it to friends.

Most Africans, however, expressed serious concern and apprehension about female genital mutilation. They all asked one question, "What are we going to do?" Some suggested openly talking about it, with the hope that it will make people become more conscious of it, increasing awareness. Others suggested an overwhelming education of the public that will involve "daughters of the soil," with lots of examples to prove that infant mortality can be caused by dirty practices and even by laying children on their stomach, causing sudden infant death. It is the African belief that an evil spirit can enter a child who lays supine on his/her back. (Laying a child on his/her back reduces the risk of Sudden Infant Death Syndrome, or SIDS.) One of the interviewees expressed concern that even if the women were convinced that circumcision does not lead to infant mortality, they would still fear that if the clitoris is not cut off their daughters will become prostitutes without husbands, which is considered a big social disgrace.

Female genital mutilation is a very big problem. It cannot be done without the father's consent or, where there is no father, without an uncle's or other male relative's consent. The consent has to come from a man. No family is compelled to circumcise their females. In a family where there is no male representative (though rare), then the consent has to come from a woman who has reached menopause; because she no longer menstruates she is considered a man and can now perform some male tasks, including pouring libations to the ancestors. If one's daughter is not circumcised, one is teased, and the daughter is ridiculed, called names, referred to as a man with a "prick." The clitoris is seen as the woman's "penis." The girl is asked, "How long is your "prick?" If she wears a pair of pants (trousers), people make a conscious effort to look "down there" to see if her clitoris is protruding through her pants. To avoid this ridicule, even some educated fathers give their consent. It doesn't matter if the child's mother protests. Some educated women who have even lived overseas, in the process of trying to become mothers (after a long search), opt to be circumcised in order to become pregnant. Female genital mutilation is indeed a very serious problem.

"Hello, is anyone out there with suggestions or possible solutions?"

Chapter Nine

The African Man and Household Chores

The African man treats his foreign wife totally different from the way he treats his African wife. He tends to understand the difference in the cultures. (Even at work, he is quicker to respond to helping a foreign woman than helping his own African sister.) Though he demands less from his foreign wife, he still thinks she is inferior. He sees her as a woman, a fourth-class citizen, because in his culture, the males come before the females. First the husband, second his brothers, third his sons, all before his wife. His expectations of the foreign wife are not totally different. He still expects her to kowtow to his whims and caprices.

Because of the way males were (and still are) brought up, with high-self esteem, the African man does not do any household chores. His mother or his sister does everything, including washing his underwear for him. He neither does the dishes, nor cooks, nor irons his own clothes. If his family does not do these things, he has many women who will be flattered if he asked them.

So when he marries a foreign wife, he expects her to do these things; if she does not, there is friction. Asking him to feed his child or to change his child's diaper or to make the bed he lays in is demeaning. It is like taking something away from his manhood. He feels belittled and insulted. He cannot understand why the wife is passing her "job" to him. If he so much as reports this to his family members, the wife will be in trouble because they, the family members, will be infuriated beyond words. "How daring . . . who does she think she is?" they will ask. If a mother is not at home, rather than prepare something to eat, both the husband and children will starve, because the husband will not know what to do. It is common to see in the African household where a husband and a wife go to work at the same time, and return home at the same time, for the man to expect his wife to prepare his food, clean the house, and do other household chores, while he sits down, tie off, shoes tossed all over (expecting his wife to pick up after him), watching TV and barking, "Where is the food? Is the food not ready yet? Why is it taking so long? Am I going to eat today? Oh, my God." He does not think that his wife may be as tired as he is; all he thinks about is his stomach. This situation made Tasha, an American formerly married to an African, ask, "Don't they have common sense?" The man does not do this out of malice. That is just the way it is. In his mind, a woman is never tired. "Why should a woman be tired? Household chores are simple, it's nothing, it's no job." That is what the men say. The African wife will try to pacify the husband by giving such husband a previously prepared homemade snack immediately when they arrive home, while she prepares the real food for the whole family. Even when a wife is sick, the husband expects her to prepare his food; he will not eat the food prepared by a maid, because he is "the man."

Not until I gave birth did I realize how painful and stressful it could be, because in Africa, when a wife gives birth, the husband does not help in any way. When the baby cries at night, the husband gets mad at the wife. Screaming, he will say, "You and your baby will not even let me sleep." Then he will walk out of the room, slamming the door behind him.

The new mother is expected to resume her normal household chores immediately, such as fetching water from the well, carrying a heavy calabash of water from the stream, washing clothes, cooking, bathing her younger children, entertaining her guests. The list is endless. This is a very dangerous practice indeed. A woman who just gave birth may develop a lot of complications. For starters, her hemoglobin (iron), which gives her strength, is low, so over-exertion could make her faint, be light-headed. She could pass out, fall, hit her head, and die on the spot. "Do the men know this? How many women have lost their lives this way?" I sometimes wonder. If the wife shows any sign of tiredness or weakness, she is branded lazy. No one takes individual differences into consideration. The man asks his wife, "If my mother can be up and about after delivery, why can't you?" Even in the hospital, the female nurses (whom one would have expected some empathy from) don't help. When a woman is in labor pain and she cries excessively, gesturing in pain and screaming at the top of her lungs, some of the nurses say to her, "Are you the first to experience labor pain? Shut up your mouth!" Excuse me, are there laws here to regulate how nurses talk to patients?

Chapter Ten

Husband's Death and Wife's Responsibilities

The average African man is very superstitious and suspicious of his family. He is not conscious of his diet. Having lived abroad for a while, Jerome became conscious of his diet. When he visited his village, he tried to educate the people on the effect of too much salt and too much oil. Says Jerome, "The people fry everything, fried egg, fried meat, fried fish, and they eat all parts of the meat, including the fats." So Jerome gathered the people together and he began, "Too much salt increases the risk

99

of hypertension. Fats are bad for you; they contain too much oil, and oil increases your bad cholesterol, which could lead to heart attack, which . . ." At this point the Community Head stopped him. The Head asked, "Who are you to tell us what and what not to eat. It is this food that we fed you before you went overseas. It is this food that our fathers' generations have been eating. Did the white man send you to tell us the food is not good for us? You go tell the white man that it is his salt that causes hypertension, not our salt. Tell him this food he says is not good keeps us alive, that we live long enough to see our great-great-great-grandchildren."

Turning to his people the Head asked, "Can someone live any longer?" The people chorused, "No!" Turning to Jerome, he said, "And you, Jero, your great-grandfather is still alive. Have you seen him eat without oil one day? How can you say that oil is bad? Can soup be enticing without oil? Or can meat be tasteful without fat? Don't you know that if the white man does not know the cause of a disease he gives it a big name? You are telling us that the oil we have been eating for generations causes *cholescholes*—what is so called? You better sit down and eat like a human being," concluded the Head. Says Jerome, "I felt like hiding." Other people told stories of similar experiences when they tried to make family members, friends and their community conscious of their diet and their looks.

Due to polygamy, the man believes that some of his wives do "juju," that is, voodoo, to get his attention.

According to the men, juju can be done in a variety of ways. Some claim that it can be put in the man's food; others claim that it can be put in the man's drink; yet others claim that it can be put in the vagina, so that when the man sleeps with the woman he will constantly have the urge to be with her and only her. In this culture when a man's sexual desire decreases before the age of retirement (sixty), he blames the wife, attributing this to voodoo. Impotence is never discussed; it is regarded as a shame, a disgrace, and therefore must be denied and blamed on the woman. If a man cannot "get it up," it is the woman's fault. She is "unclean." She has done voodoo, some men even say, "because she does not turn me on." But it has been medically proven that men's sexual desire naturally decreases between the ages of forty and fifty-five, some earlier than others. Some doctors call it "manopause." Just as women experience changes in their bodies as they age called menopause, so also the man experiences changes. This "manopause" happens with age and decrease in physical activities. Impotence is no shame; it is no disgrace. There are vitamins, medications and herbs both to treat impotence and to increase sexual desires. If you are experiencing "manopause," please ask for help. Do not be ashamed.

When the African husband is sick, rather than seek professional medical advice, he seeks the advice of psychics known as *Ogbebunu*, that is, native doctors, in order to find out who amongst his wives is trying to kill him. Most of the time the psychic, not wanting to appear stupid, will pick a name from the list submitted to him. Such a woman will not only be sent packing, her children and generations after her will be labeled forever. Due to the "voodoo" belief, it becomes difficult for one to know the medical history of one's family. Here the death of anyone is always associated with witchcraft or an inexplicable "magic." The popular reaction is, *dem done kill am*.

When a husband (or any one) dies, no autopsy is done, for fear that his body parts will not be complete when he reincarnates. His wife is deprived of eating between seven and twenty-one days, depending on the culture, as a sign of respect for the dead husband. During this period, she is deprived of a bath and decent clothing. She is allowed to wear only black, dirty, tattered clothing. She is made to dig the earth with her fingers as a sign of her innocence, that she did not kill her husband. In Edo State, to say goodbye to her husband, the wife is made to suffocate a live chicken in between her thighs and to use the dead chicken to go round her head seven times, throwing the chicken behind her, at the seventh count, without looking behind her. The belief is that if she looks back, the dead husband's spirit will haunt her forever. At the end of this compulsory fasting, she is made to eat with her left (dirty) fingers. If during this period she falls sick, it is automatically assumed that her dead husband wants her to join him. No treatment or any medical attention of any kind will be given to her. No one cares about the poor environmental condition that she has been exposed to. If, however, she dies during this period or develops any open area or sores, she will not be buried; she will be thrown into the forest to be eaten up by animals, because it is assumed that her dead husband has sought vengeance for his death.

When a husband dies, his whole properties automatically go to his extended family members. The wives are treated as part of his properties and shared as his other properties. Firstborn sons are very important. The ordinal position of the son does not matter; he may be the man's lastborn, but as long as he is the first son, he automatically has authority over the girls. The late man's wives are given to the sons, the brothers, or the cousins to marry. (Mothers and sons do not marry each other, but mothers are given to step-sons to marry.) If any of the wives refuses, she will be cursed and isolated and thrown out of the husband's compound. The extended family members, however, sell the properties and share the money among themselves without giving anything to the wives and children. "Wills" are not respected in this culture. "What is so called?" the folks will ask. They call it un-African, a borrowed culture.

Firstborn males are sometimes given part of their father's properties. Most of the time, these first sons sell the properties in secret, with or without papers or deeds. Sometimes these properties are sold to more than one person. This is especially common today in the country due to the hardship the people are facing. A few Nigerians abroad have had a taste of the hassle of having to deal with one landed property being sold to several people. In a situation like this, the court will have to decide who the real owner of the property is, and this takes a long time. The people abroad will end up losing because of time and distance.

Jokpa, a reputable artist, lived in London for fifteen years. Says Jokpa, "I just got burnt out living there. I got tired of the hassle and all. I wanted to go back to my people. I missed the home life." So Jokpa gathered all he had saved since his arrival in London and went home to his people. He bought a very big piece of land. He intended to use part of the land for business and the other part for residence. It was very well designed by an architect. Half-way through the completion of the building, a group of men came to the builders to ask what they were doing. The builders were confused. "Who are you?" asked the head builder. "You don't know?" crassly answered the shortest of them all, thick set, receding hair with red and fiery eyes. "No," answered the head builder, with all the workers watching in anticipation. Behold, when the short guy called his name, the whole place went quiet. According to Jokpa, "You could have heard a pin drop." This was the most dreaded man in town; he had a terrible reputation. He kills whoever crosses his path. Jokpa then stepped forward and introduced himself and asked, "Can we talk?" The man had bought the land three years prior to when the same person sold the land to Jokpa. Mr. "Shorty" had proof of purchase.

Jokpa said, "I didn't know what to do. So many things went through my mind. Why didn't this man come when I laid the foundation. Why now? I had put so much money into this building. Should I give it up without a fight? Instantly, I made a decision. 'I will go to court and fight for my property.' As if the man read my thoughts, he said, 'Young man, I do not go to court. I am ordering you and your boys to get out of my property. I give you two weeks to take away your structure, after that, I will tear it down. Good day.' Mr. 'Shorty' walked away. I was confused. I knew he meant what he had said. I went to my mother, who accompanied me to the Head of the Community, who then invited Mr. 'Shorty' for a meeting."

At this point, I stopped Jokpa and asked why he did not go to his father. "Why go to your mother? After all, your father is a man like Mr. 'Shorty.'" Jokpa replied, "Pat, this is a very serious matter. My life savings was on the line. All I had worked hard for was about to go down the drain just like that" (snapping his fingers). Then he continued: "I know my father. He would want to fight fire with fire. Rather than talk this through gently, he would challenge the man, and I tell you, I was not about to watch all my family get killed because of a piece of property."

I stopped him again and asked, "So you thought your mother had the solution." He continued: "That's right. I have always trusted my mother's instinct. I would have done whatever she had advised I do. Mama wanted to keep this between us until it was resolved." "So what happened?" I asked. Jokpa narrated: "I stopped building at the site. Mr. 'Shorty' did come to the community meeting on the set date, accompanied by a long entourage of guests. As if my mama had anticipated this, she had prepared a variety of menus with her meeting members in tow to serve. One would think I was getting married." Jokpa chuckled. "Anyway, Mama went to Mr. 'Shorty,' genuflected, and introduced herself as my mother, and without being asked, Mama started telling the history of her lineage. In one swift breath, Mama had linked ten generations together, just like that." He snapped his fingers again. "At this point, Mr. 'Shorty' ordered, 'Stop!' My heart skipped a beat. Oh, God! what has my mama done? Who asked her about her lineage? I pondered and waited. Mr. 'Shorty' then stood up, looked at my mother for about five seconds and shook his head. Everyone was quiet, waiting. The eating had stopped. The Head of the Community, who summoned the meeting, was confused. My heart was beating so fast I thought I was going to have a heart attack. Then Mr. 'Shorty' said, 'Sit down, my sister.'

"What? Did I hear right? I looked from one face to the other. I saw the same expression as mine, unbelievable. Mr. 'Shorty' continued: 'It is good to know one's lineage. In a minute, Jopka's mother has given her son a life. Even though I respected the Community Head by being here today, he would not have been able to change my mind. I meant what I said when I asked Jopka to remove his structure from my land. Yes, I was aware of the foundation. I would have stopped the building then, but I wanted to punish the boy from overseas to prove that with his education and money, he is nothing. But that boy from overseas is my son. How can one punish one's own son?'

Mr. 'Shorty' then went on to tell how he and my mother were related. They turned out to be seventh cousins. Turning to me, he said, 'For your mother's sake, young man, I will allow you to buy back my land from me.' Everyone thanked him, and the eating resumed."

Jopka stopped and sighed with relief as if the incident had just happened. I asked if his father ever got to know what happened and, if so, what was his reaction. Jokpa said his father was livid with anger (after the fact), that his father didn't think he should buy back the land and attempted to take the money back from Mr. "Shorty," but backed down when Mr. "Shorty" threatened to take back his "sister" from him.

Some people, however, are not so lucky. They lose their lives because of landed properties or houses. Sometimes mothers and siblings will find out about the sold properties when the buyer evicts them in order to assume his new property. Who can one trust?

Chapter Eleven

The Joy of Poverty

No one is born into this world with wealth. Everyone comes here in their "birthday suit"—naked, pure and simple. Some people are born into greatness and affluence, others are born poor and achieve greatness, yet others are born poor, accept their condition, and blame nature for being so unkind to them. The latter set of people often ask the question, "Why me?"

It is a myth to think or believe that everyone in the African continent lives in poverty. Oh, what ignorance to think that all homes in Africa are "huts" or "cottages" or that Africa is a "jungle." The African continent—North, South, East and West—is abundantly rich in natural resources. Everything and anything that makes life comfortable for Americans and other advanced countries can be found in Africa. Aircraft, tarred roads, electricity, computers, microwaves, washing machines/driers, dishwashers, refrigerators, stoves, cars, fantastic buildings that one can only dream of seeing in Hollywood pictures are all there.

An American colleague once asked me if I had ever seen a live elephant. I answered, "Yes, in the zoo and at the circus show." Immediately, she burst into a tirade of laughter. I was surprised and puzzled. "Why are you laughing?" I asked. She answered, "How can you, an African, claim to have only seen a live elephant in the zoo or at the circus?" She burst into another bout of laughter, then she asked, "Do you in Africa have any other form of transportation apart from animals?" Other American colleagues started laughing. They thought it was funny, but it wasn't funny to me. I walked away. I remembered a favorite saying of my mama, "You ignore the ignorant."

One of my nieces-in-law once asked me, "Isn't it wonderful that my uncle has introduced you to wearing clothes?" "What do you mean?" I asked. She replied, "Oh, you Africans do not put on clothes, we see that on TV all the time." Boy! I couldn't believe it. Here is an African American referring to me as "you African." I laughed. I asked her, "Are you not an African?" She said "No, I am an American." Rather than ignore her, I proceeded to educate her. I explained that she is an African born in America, and that being born in America does not mean that she has lost her identity. My niece was puzzled. She asked, "If all that you have told me about Africa is right, if Africa is as beautiful as you described, why don't they show us on TV?" I could not answer that. I once said to my husband, Ernest, "I can't wait to take you to Nigeria to give you a good time." My husband responded, "If you call dancing around the fireplace a good time." Though Ernest later said he was joking, I would have excused him even if he wasn't joking, not because he is my husband, but because a majority of the motion pictures he has seen in the past, coupled with the pictures of the dilapidated condition of my home in Africa, enhanced the impression of what he thinks Africa is like. My husband has never been to Africa.

Even though Africa has all the comfortable amenities that the advanced countries have, not everyone can afford them. My family happens to be one of such. I grew up in an under-privileged background, though at the time neither I nor my siblings felt under-privileged. Even though my home was not beautiful materially, to me it was (and still is) the best place to be on earth. My mother was very loving and dedicated. Like a typical African mother, she put her life on hold to raise her children, very committed to motherhood. She was very generous in providing the very best for her children. I had one senior brother, one senior sister, three younger sisters, and one younger brother. My senior brother and sister were already away from home by the time I was in college. I had three other senior brothers and one senior sister who were my father's children who were not living with us but were constantly visiting. All my senior sisters and brothers were highly placed in various professions—the military, customs, banks, immigrations, and teaching. My home was and still is full of love, support, and encouragement. We were told "the sky is your limit . . . you can be anything you want to be."

As children we lacked nothing. As teenagers, it was fun going from one sibling to the other to gather money to pay school fees. We soon learned to differentiate between needs and wants, to be prudent and save for the "rainy day." We learned to put up with and accept disappointments as a way of life. We learned that trust is earned, that the only ones you can trust are members of your nuclear family, that some uncles and cousins cannot be trusted. We soon learned to differentiate between sincerity and deceit. During my time at home money was hard to come by; therefore, to make ends meet, one extended financial request to some uncles and or cousins who on several occasions, rather than deny the request, would ask that one come on a certain day; when that day would come, they would say "come tomorrow," and so on, until finally one figured out that the uncle or cousin did not want to help. At first this realization hits you like a bang! You cry. But repeated disappointments like this make you tough and you soon accept it as a way of life, a gamble, win or lose; either way, it's okay, life goes on. You say to yourself, "If one road closes, another road opens." You wipe your tears and go looking for the other road. Instinctively, you know how to approach an individual, you learn manners. You learn from facial expressions whether to tell the purpose of your visit—which is to ask for financial assistance or to say you are on a courtesy visit. We knew we could not afford to fail. The price, both financially and emotionally, was too high.

Africans believe in giving, though there are some stingy people. When a mother goes to a party, she takes a souvenir home to her children because she wants her children to be a part of the party. The African mother may not hug her children everyday, she may not say to her children, "I love you," everyday, but the child knows that he/she is loved. The mother's actions more than prove it. The majority of Africans give freely because they believe that there is an intangible and unlimited blessing in giving. The African woman, especially, practices the act of giving. She gives generously from the heart. She never complains; rather, she is thankful that she is able to help. Says my sister Elizabeth, "It could be worse, you know. The people could be suffering without one being able to help. Thank God one is able. My bill can wait." She concluded with, "Give, and it shall be given unto you in abundance." This is how many African women reason.

The African woman will spend less money buying material things in order to save enough money to care for extended family members. She likes to look good, she dresses to match, but she knows that "expensive" does not mean "superior." Some African women overseas buy things on "sale," not because they cannot afford the real price, but because they have "plenty" mouths to feed.

(The sad part of this is that all the money being sent to their home countries is not tax-deductible because these dependents do not have Social Security numbers.) Amaka, a nutritionist, asked, "Why should I buy an out-fit for three hundred dollars, when that three hundred dollars, if converted to Nigerian currency, will pay my sister's school fees for a year?" Amaka's question reminded me of what my mama used to say when we were growing up: "To everything there is a time. When that time comes, you will buy that outfit no matter how expensive." Mama would conclude with, "First things first." It's okay to buy expensive things if one can afford it, but buying things on sale to save money in order to help others is being real, not cheap!

In Africa, sometimes when a man offers to buy a woman a drink, she may say to him, "Give me the money instead." Though she may not tell the man what she wants to do with the money, she is not going to use the money for herself; she is going to use the money to put food on the table for her people. Some people may ask, "Why doesn't she just say to him, 'Give me the money to buy food for my siblings'?" Because apart from "woman's pride," that singular statement is enough to make the man "take off," because some men are vain, craving to belong where they do not belong. They will spend thousands of dollars to buy an outfit just to show off, even if it means not having fuel (gas) in their cars or not having food in the home. They will spend "bor-rowed" money just to impress a woman. They are class conscious, wanting to reap where they did not sow.

When I was teaching, I witnessed many promising young girls whose hearts were broken by men because the girls did not come from the "right" socio-economic background. Some of these girls could not be consoled, some of them cursed their poverty, others cursed the day they were born, yet others fully recovered, a few recovering faster than others. I could relate to the experiences of these girls because I have been there. When I was in college, I had a similar experience (which I considered positive) with Sylvanax, an engineer from a similar humble background as me, the only educated child in the midst of five sisters and a brother. Sylvanax and I got along well, or so I thought, until he accompanied me to my home. Thereafter, Sylvanax started behaving funny. I never read any meaning into his weird behavior, but I was worried. I contacted his friend whom I call *Egbon* (brother). I asked, "Egbon, what's the matter with your friend? I have not seen nor heard from him, I am worried." Egbon paused, looked at me with that "I'm sorry" look, then cleared his throat and said, "Patsy, I do not know how to say this." But his expression said it all. I even had a feeling that Sylvanax was hiding somewhere in that house. I responded, "Egbon, say it." Egbon hesitated, then cleared his throat again, looked behind him as if asking for help, then took a deep breath, releasing his breath very slowly, and began, "Patsy, you are beautiful. You are a smart and intelligent girl. Sylvanax loves you. He really cares for you, he . . ." I was beginning to lose my patience. I interrupted, "Cut the crap, go straight to the point." I realized too late that I sounded harsher than

I intended, but I did not apologize. Egbon glared at me, but I looked away, waiting. He sighed then as quickly as he could, as if afraid his courage would fail him, and said, "It's over, Patsy." "What's the reason he gave you?" I inquired. But Egbon wouldn't respond. "Please, tell me," I pleaded. Egbon tightened his lips together, but said nothing.

But I wouldn't give up. This is the African style. The African woman never gives up what she started; when she sets her mind on something, she will climb walls to achieve it. She will not use force; she uses her femininity to get what she needs. "Two wrongs don't make a right," the African child is told. She will modulate her voice to suit the situation. I probed further. With a wintry smile, I asked as sweetly as I could, "Egbon, is there anything that your sister cannot handle? Please tell me." Egbon turned away from me, supporting his neck with his left open palm, tilting his head slightly to the left, still not looking at me, and said with a quivering voice, "It's your background, Patsy." Then turning to me, he continued, "Sylvanax thinks you have too many responsibilities." I think Egbon misconstrued my lack of response and quiet demeanor for sadness, for he continued, "Patsy, Sylvanax really loves you." For the first time in my life, I looked at a man straight in the eye. I said, "Don't you say that Sylvanax loves me again. If he loved me, he would love everything about me, no matter how poor." With tears in my eyes, I walked away.

On my way, I asked myself a lot of questions. "Where did I go wrong? What gave Sylvanax the impression that I have too many responsibilities, especially since I have never asked him for a penny? What does he know about me? Was I wrong to have taken him to my family home? We owned the home; was it because the home was old? Why should I be ashamed of where I was brought up? Why couldn't he accept me as I am?" Then I remembered what Mama used to say when we were growing up: "There is more to life than wealth. If someone does not accept you as you are, then that person is not worth being your friend." Instantly, I was consoled. Then I remembered my grandmother's favorite saying, "I, Leleji (Dedi), the daughter of Ohiambe of Amukpe origin, say to you this day, remove bitterness from your heart so that you will be able to move on in life." Instantly, I had inner peace. As children we used to joke with Dedi's saying, but this day it made sense. Indeed, bitterness has no place in the mind of the African woman. "What good will depression do?" the African mother will ask a sad one. "Depression leads to destruction. Wipe away your tears, eat, get up, and go. Tomorrow is another day," the African mother will console.

In Africa when one sibling is sad, everyone is sad; when one sibling grieves, everyone grieves; when one sibling is happy, everyone is happy. I remember when I went through my divorce, it was like the whole family was experiencing divorce. At one point, my ex became a subject of riddles and jokes. Family members would ask, "What did you see in that ugly man?" My brothers would tease, "I bet he has a short prick." At this, all of us girls would scream and bury our faces in our hands. Yet another would say, "There must be holes in his underwear," and another, "That man farts too much." Here I was thinking my world was over, yet I never laughed so hard. At one point, I came to my ex's defense. At this point, Mama said, "Okay, everyone, let this matter be. Patience is healed." Indeed I was healed. In retrospect, God had a purpose for that divorce. Today, I have a sincere husband who loves and respects me, who thinks the world of me, who treats me like a queen. I love him, too. To everything there is a purpose.

Life in Africa is beautiful. The stress level is different. Looking back today, the best time of my life was when I was a child. "They say what you don't know you don't miss." They also say, "In the land of the blind, the one-eyed man is the king." In my community, my family was the one-eyed man. We were the "privileged" among the under-privileged. Where other families were renting, we owned our home. Where children were sleeping on the floor, we were sleeping on the bed. Where people were trekking miles to fetch water from the stream/river, we had a well in our compound and a water tap (pump) nearby. Where families were sharing notebooks, each of us had a notebook for each subject.

In elementary school, it was a privilege to get a new uniform. The uniform was sewn very big so that you grew into it. You use one uniform for years. You keep your uniform very neat, otherwise, not only will you be labeled "dirty pig," the teachers will *bulala* (whip) your butt so hard that you will only be able to sit on the side of your butt for days. You learn to dry and wash one uniform twice a week and as needed. If your uniform gets wrinkled, you are in trouble with the teacher's bulala. If you don't have an iron, you wake up very early in the morning and spread your uniform in the morning *itoto* (morning dew). The coal iron we had in the family was used by those in high school. Those of us in the elementary school used the "dew" iron. The dew was very kind and loving. She removed the wrinkles and gave the uniform a very cool and comforting feeling so that it felt good and soothing to the skin.

Cockcrow was the natural "alarm" because clocks and wristwatches were luxuries. Most homes had none, but you dare not come late to school for fear of the teacher's bulala. Even though we had no wristwatches, we learned to tell the time of day by merely looking at the weather. We knew when it would rain or storm by merely noticing the change of weather or by looking at the position of the sun. (The moon provided a soothing environment for storytelling.)

Being well groomed from head to toe was a must, not a choice. For some reason, the bottom of my uniform would always age more than the top, so you would find me wearing a new bottom attached to an old top. Boy, was I proud and confident! My shoes were always at least two sizes too big, stuffed with cotton wool to fit. I used one pair of school sandals for years. The sole of the shoe was protected with *kakaro*. I was privileged to wear shoes. A majority of the pupils went to school bare footed. At the time, most children only wore shoes during festivals, like Christmas and New Years. During sports, however, our games masters made every child participate barefooted because the oversized shoes were hindering our abilities to perform. A majority of us children had shoemakers as friends. If perchance your shoe strap got cut by accident or due to "old age," you quickly went to your shoemaker friend to fix it. Or if your big toe began to protrude or leave an indented mark on your shoes, you'd take it to your shoemaker friend to patch.

Parents never interfered with education. Every pupil was serious at school. Teachers were prompt and consistent. Teachers marked and redistributed all homework to pupils. Every morning, immediately after the morning assembly, there was the "mental" test, a quiz comprising twenty questions, done in five minutes. This test was designed to test the cognition, one's ability to remember. The quiz was divided into two parts—Mathematics (comprising all science subjects) and English (comprising the arts). The test did not encourage rote memory. The Friday mental test was the most dreaded because the test was drawn from all one had done since the beginning of the week, including one's homework. Every pupil was expected to pass the English test with one hundred percent accuracy, but the girls were expected to pass the Mathematics test with forty percent accuracy. All pupils were apprehensive at the distribution of the answers to the test questions, because if you fail one question out of twenty questions, you get one whip, the more questions you fail, the more *bulala* you get. Pupils were made to stand up before the distribution of the answers. The teacher would command, "Twenty-twenty, sit!" This meant that all pupils who got all twenty answers right were to sit down. Those concerned would sit down. The whole class would be made to applaud such pupils. Clapping was the greatest form of motivation. Then the teacher would command, "Nineteen-twenty, come out!" Those who got one answer wrong would come out. The teacher would bulala their butt one time, with a warning to get all twenty questions right next time. God help you if you got nothing right, that is "zero-twenty." Everyone in the class will be asked to "shame" you and call you *Olo-oh*, which means a dull and unintelligent individual. The whole class would chant, "sha-a-me on you, Olo-do-oh." Then you would be made to lie prone (stomach facing down) on the teacher's table with your head tucked in between your outstretched arms, both legs outstretched, while the teacher bulala your backside with a vengeance. If you complained to your parents about the teacher's whip, your parents would ask, "If your mate could get twenty-twenty, why couldn't you?"

After school, most parents made provision for "lesson" teachers. Any pupil who did not measure up to the standard was made to repeat the class. Such a pupil was nicknamed *failly-failly*. This was a stigma. No pupil wanted to be stigmatized, so every pupil studied hard. However, desperation soon led to invention. Not knowing what to expect every morning, some pupils soon devised a method of tolerating the teacher's bulala. This was called "loading." Loading involved padding the butt unnoticeably with cloth to serve as cushion to absorb the whip. One boy new to "loading" loaded his butt so much so that his teacher became suspicious. The teacher asked, "Yesterday your butt was flat. How did it get so big today?" It is important to note that bulala has since been discouraged in schools. On the whole, however, learning was fun. Our imagination was stretched beyond limit. Even though we had no real audiovisual aids, no calculators, no telephone, no computers, no TV, the standard of education and pupil's performance was high, and very well correlated.

At the time, even though we didn't know it, there were some advantages to being poor and unexposed: pure and unadulterated innocence. A mother says to her child, "Do not eat someone else's food." Someone else (maybe the aunt or the uncle) offers the child food, and even in the face of hunger, the child says, "My mama says not to eat someone else's food," and the child will not eat. A tired mother says to her children, "I am going to sleep. If anyone asks for me, say 'I am not at home.'" A visitor asks, "Is your mama home?" The child says, "My mama says for us to say that she is not at home, but she is in the bedroom. I bet she could hear you, too. She couldn't have fallen asleep so fast." Then the child may call out, "Mama, can you hear me?" The tired mama is forced to come out.

Poverty teaches you to appreciate the little you have. It discourages you from taking what is not yours. There is nowhere to hide what you stole. Every sibling knows what every sibling has up to the color of the pen. Any new thing is brought to the attention of the parents, who will investigate the source. God help you if you stole! Stealing is intolerable. Even if you took money from your mama's *okugbe* (waist pocket), it is called stealing, and your mama will expose you. Mothers pay attention. They know the things that each child is capable of doing. So if a mother loses a penny from her okugbe, she knows who took it. Siblings tell on siblings. Lying is discouraged, honesty encouraged by praises, by getting an extra piece of meat or fish. It is believed that a child who lies will end up being a thief or a prostitute, and this was (and still is) considered a big social disgrace. A child who steals is made to go through the *Ole-Nole-Jankonico* Therapy. Every child dreaded this therapy. This therapy is administered when it is determined that the child is old enough to know the difference between good and bad, right and wrong, usually from the formative years and up to the age of twelve.

A child who steals is called "Ole" or "Tify-Tify." This is the local name for a thief. During the Ole-Nole-Jankonico Therapy, Tify-Tify's face is blackened with ground charcoal and snail shells are tied around his/her waist. Jingle bells are tied around both ankles. His age-mates line up behind him and begin to sing and clap their hands, "Ole-Nole-Jankonico . . . Oyo . . . yo." Whatever the child stole will automatically become part of the song. If he stole money, the song becomes, "Tify-Tify money, oyo . . . yo, Ole-Nole-Jankonico, oyo . . . yo." Tify-Tify is made to go around all the public places in town—his school, the library, hospital and the market place. As Tify-Tify walks along with his age mates in tow, his jingle bells attract more crowds, adults and children alike. Everyone will be clapping and singing, "Ole-Nole-Jankonico, oyo . . . yo." As they sing, the child is made to dance to the music. At intervals, the crowd will stop and ask, *"Tify-Tify, you go thief again?"* (Will you steal again?) The child responds, "No." The crowd chants "louder." Tify-Tify says "No" louder. The crowd continues to chant "louder" until Tify-Tify begins to cry and say repeatedly, *"I nor go steal again"* (I will not steal again).

This Ole-Nole-Jankonico Therapy is a very long therapy. The session may take a whole day. When the child has gone to all the public places in town, he/she is then returned home, and his/her age mates are dismissed. After this therapy, no one mentions this incident again. It is over. The child has paid for his/her sins; he/she is forgiven. In all the cases I observed, stealing was never repeated. Some of those involved turned out to be high ranking professionals. One of them (my classmate) became a medical doctor. He returned to the community to serve. He became a strong proponent of this Ole-Nole-Jankonico Therapy. Says the Doc, "If not for this therapy, who knows what I would have become."

Poverty teaches you teamwork and brings about unity in the family. It also teaches you how to get "bullies"off your back. You know that you are all you've got, you stick together—united we stand, divided we fall. You soon discover that there is strength and power in numbers. If you hurt one person, you'd better be ready to hurt them all. At the time, to show your strength, you fight physically with your fist. To date, Africans still believe that only lazy people carry weapons, that a real man fights with the fist. A family of mostly girls soon learns to fight like men, setting blows and using their elbows to *colobee* (attack the carotid pressure area).

I could go on and on about the advantages of poverty; the life experiences that being poor teaches cannot be bought. If there is any individual out there who was or still is disappointed because of his/her under-privileged or poor background, take heart. Poverty is no crime. Poverty is no shame. Poverty is no disgrace. No one controls his/her birthplace. If anyone could determine his/her birthplace, no one would want to be born poor. Poverty is a challenge. Some rich people today were born poor yesterday. Poverty enables one to turn obstacles into opportunities. Do not run away from poverty. Face it and conquer it. Running away solves no problems. You are already down. The only place for you to go is up. As one of my elementary rhymes goes:

> I go up . . .
>
> up, up I go.

Poverty never goes away. It is a constant reminder of life. One could be rich today and be poor tomorrow. Fight poverty! Don't let poverty put you down. Why feel sorry for yourself? There are as many opportunities out there as there are people. Look around you and bloom where you are. The trees yonder are not always greener. You are stronger and more creative than you think.

Poverty, however, becomes a curse and a setback if you sit down and accept it, wallowing in self-pity, if you are content with your position, looking at TV daily, wishing to be like so-and-so, drinking and drugging your life away, hoping against hope that someday someone will rescue you. The truth is, no one will. If you want to be rescued, you've got to rescue yourself first. Do not wait for opportunity to come to you; go looking for the opportunity. You never know what you might find. Yes, you may come across obstacles; you may come across disappointment upon disappointment. You may even be ridiculed, but do not give up. Bitter experiences are meant to make us better people. As my grandmother Dedi usually says, "Remove bitterness from your heart and practice forgiveness so that you can move on." Do not fear to ask. Fear itself is an obstacle. As they say in Africa, "No venture, no success." When you ask, you will get either of two responses, "Yes" or "No," but neither response will come if you are too afraid to try. And you know what? The response is between you and the responder; the answer is not written on your forehead. No one else knows. As Daddy often asks, "So what if you are turned down, is that the end of life?" And he concludes with, "Try! Try! Try! When you stay long enough in the dark, you will begin to see." It is time for you to see. Come on! Get up and go! Let's fight poverty!

Epilogue

In the process of writing this book, I sometimes found myself being the interviewee. One question I was commonly asked was, "Pat, you have tasted both the foreign and the African world; which do you prefer?" Inasmuch as I do not voice out any opinion, especially as my research in this area is limited at this time, one question I ask in reply is, "Which will you prefer, a man who beats you up and kisses away your tears, or a man who womanizes?" **No one is perfect.** A good man is a good man anywhere in the world. If you find one, keep him. As my brother Group Captain Ewere Okundaye always says, "If you follow human weaknesses, you will have no friends."

For ordering information call or write to:

Turtoe-Sanders Communications Company
P.O.Box 43481
Brooklyn Park, MN 55443
Phone: (612) 561-5585
E-mail: nyphen@aol.com